SCHOLASTIC

Pie Corbett

Storyteller

Traditional tales to read, tell and write

Terms and conditions: CD-Rom

IMPORTANT – PERMITTED USE AND WARNINGS · READ CAREFULLY BEFORE USING

Minimum specification:
- PC or Mac with a 16x CD-Rom drive and 256 Mb RAM
- Windows 98 or higher
- Mac OSX 10.1.5 or higher
- Recommended minimum processor speed: 800 MHz
- 16bit sound and graphics card

For all technical support queries, please phone Scholastic Customer Services on 0845 6039091.

Nine stories to watch on CD-Rom

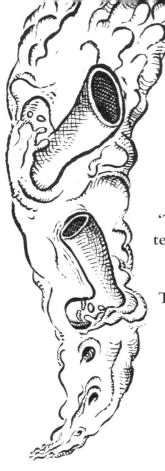

Credits

'This series is dedicated to all those parents, storytellers and teachers who keep the flame of stories alive in children's minds.'
Pie Corbett

The publishers would like to thank the children and staff at Ebrington, Grasmere and South Grove Primary Schools for their help in creating this product.

Author
Pie Corbett

Editor
Sarah Snashall

Development Editors
Simret Brar / Rachel Mackinnon

Cover Illustration
© Steve Lavis / Bright Agency

Illustrations
© Harris Sofokleous / Sylvie Poggio

Series Designer / Designer
Andrea Lewis

CD-Rom Development
Q and D Multimedia Ltd / Adrian Moss/ Atmospheres Ltd

Text © 2008 Pie Corbett
© 2008 Scholastic Ltd

Designed using Adobe InDesign

Published by Scholastic Ltd
Villiers House
Clarendon Avenue
Leamington Spa
Warwickshire
CV32 5PR

www.scholastic.co.uk

Printed by Bell and Bain Ltd
2 3 4 5 6 7 8 9   9 0 1 2 3 4 5 6 7

British Library Cataloguing-in-Publication Data
A catalogue record for this book is available from the British Library.

ISBN 978-1407-10067-8

Acknowledgements
The right of the Pie Corbett to be identified as the author of this work has been asserted by him in accordance with the Copyright, Designs and Patents Act 1988.

Contents

For ages 4 to 7

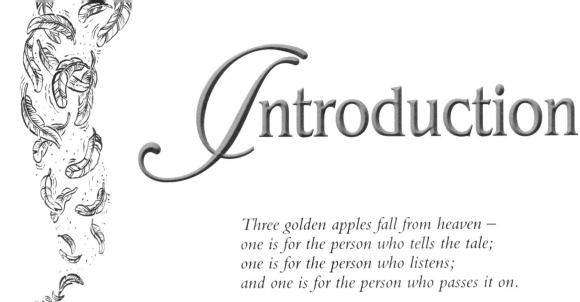

Introduction

Three golden apples fall from heaven –
one is for the person who tells the tale;
one is for the person who listens;
and one is for the person who passes it on.

About the series

Storyteller develops the spoken art of storytelling through print, audio, video and the spoken word. The series comprises for 4 to 7 year olds:

- *The Gingerbread Man and other stories* – a collection of 16 stories with an audio CD (providing all the stories read aloud).
- *Storyteller Ages 4 to 7* – teacher's notes on each story with a CD-Rom (providing videos of nine stories being told and four storytellers talking about their craft).

The aim of *Storyteller* is to provide a bank of stories that families, teachers and children might retell and develop to make their own.

Why tell stories?

Storytelling weaves a spell that binds us all into one world community. We enter that other world where anything is possible and we can think, feel and grow together. They help us to fashion who we are and to know what is right and what is wrong.

Many schools have discovered that if children learn stories orally, it improves the quality of their writing. This is because oral storytelling develops the children's self-confidence as storytellers, it provides a bank of possibilities to draw upon and encourages the flow of story language and patterns that they can use when writing. If a child knows a story really well, when they sit down to write, it makes the task of writing easier because the brain does not have to compose at the same time as tackling handwriting, spelling and punctuation.

Research has shown that children who are read to and hear stories before coming to school are the most likely to succeed in school. This is because stories help children to sit still, listen and concentrate; they also develop abstract thinking so that children who have had stories told or read to them are the first to form abstract concepts across the curriculum. In addition, stories create a comforting and imaginative world in which ogres can be confronted and our deepest fears played out and controlled.

As educationalists, we also know that children who are read to or have stories told to them begin to build up and internalise narrative possibilities. Through repetitive, memorable and meaningful storytelling, children build up:

- **The big patterns of stories** – rather like putting templates in the mind. Ted Hughes called these 'blueprints for the imagination'.

- **The building blocks of a story** – openings, dilemmas, action, suspense, resolutions as well as characters, settings and events.
- **The flow of sentences** – because story sentences are different to everyday speech. For instance, *In a distant valley lived a giant.*
- **Words** – not only descriptive language and tricks such as alliteration or imagery, but also story language such as *once upon a time*, *one day*, *unfortunately*, *luckily* and *finally*.

The conditions for internalising these narrative patterns are as follows:
- **Repetition** – the stories have to be heard not once, not twice but at least three times. Children then need time to keep retelling their version in order to gain fluency and confidence.
- **Memorable** – the stories have to be made memorable so that they stay inside the child's mind, a metaphor for their lives. This is why in the teacher's notes I have provided suggestions for artwork, drama, and other forms of exploration.
- **Meaningful** – if the language of the story is to become generative then the children have to understand what the sentences mean. Again, this is why we might paint scenes, act the story out with puppets or hot-seat characters. All of these activities help children to deepen their understanding and appreciation – as well as ensuring that the patterns can be internalised and reused as part of the child's linguistic competence.
- **Hear it** – to internalise a story, it is important that children *hear* them. This may be through the audio CD, watching the videos on the CD-Rom or having the teacher read the story aloud – or most effectively, tell the story. A good telling creates the story in the child's mind.
- **Telling it** – to internalise the story so that it becomes their own, the children have to retell it. Language is learned by 'hearing it' and then 'saying it'. Of course, they will need time to retell a tale until they have gained fluency and confidence.

On the CD-Rom you will find:

Oral performances of nine stories:

1. *The Holy Man* told by Xanthe Gresham
2. *Why Dog Lives With Man* told by Taffy Thomas
3. *The Gingerbread Man* told by Taffy Thomas
4. *Farmer Merryweather's Cow* told by Taffy Thomas
5. *The Cat's Drum* told by Taffy Thomas
6. *Greedy Fox* told by Pie Corbett
7. *The Little Red Hen* told by Pie Corbett
8. *Ananse and the Golden Box of Stories* told by Jane Grell
9. *Monkey See, Monkey Do!* told by Pie Corbett

Storytellers talking about their craft:

Pie Corbett
Xanthe Gresham
Taffy Thomas
Jane Grell

How to tell a story

Telling a story yourself

Storytelling is not as daunting as one might first imagine. We all have a natural propensity towards telling and will have told many anecdotes and recounted many events. Make storytelling easier by following these tips:

- **Choose a story** – find a tale that you like. Start with something fairly brief that has a repetitive pattern.
- **Adapt the story** – this stage is not necessary, but it definitely helps to rewrite the story that you're going to tell because it helps internalise the pattern (and build in any specific language pattern that you want the children to learn).
- **Draw a story map, board or flowchart** – this is crucial. Annotate any rhythmic patterns or special words that you must use (though keep writing to a minimum). Any pictures will help you 'see' the story in your mind.
- **Listen to it** – use the audio CD (supplied with the anthology). Listen and then join in to gain confidence. Listen to the story at least three times in order to be able to attempt a retelling.
- **Try saying the story aloud** – you can have the map in front of you, or just try to see the story in your head. Practise telling the story several times on your own.
- **Now tell it** – find a class and retell the story. You will be surprised how easy it is. Remember that you do not have to know most of the stories word for word.

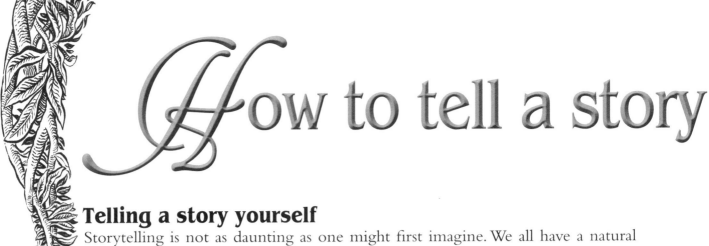

Why Dog Lives With Man story map

Illustration © Scholastic Ltd

Helping the children retell

Learning a story takes time. However, the more experienced the children become, the quicker they can learn. Storytelling improves memory. Help the children retell stories by following this process:

- **Listen to the story** – a number of times. Initially, tell the tale and then discuss likes, dislikes, puzzles and patterns.
- **Draw a story map** – ask the children to listen to the story again and draw a story map or board or a flowchart of key scenes.
- **Watch it** – watch the story on the CD-Rom. Discuss with the children what they liked about 'how' the storytellers tell their tales. Make a list of criteria for good storytelling. For example: speak clearly and loudly; vary the volume, expresssion and pace; use gestures to support the meaning. It might be interesting to compare the written and told versions, which in some cases vary considerably.

- **Activities** – undertake other activities such as drama, writing in role, art, model making, and so on. Set up the audio CD in a listening corner.
- **Join in** – retell the story and encourage the children to increasingly join in. In the end, you may have a unique class version! (With children who have English as a new language or where children struggle with speaking, learning some 'communal' tales word for word can be very helpful. You will find that each anthology has some simple tales with repetitive patterns that would lend themselves to this form of retelling. It is crucial to help the children by using actions for the key events and connectives as well as the map.)
- **Use actions** – use actions with enthusiasm to enhance events.
- **Paired retellings** – put the children in pairs and ask them to retell the tale, either together or by taking turns (they can use their maps or flowcharts). Remember, they do not have to learn the story word for word – they are developing their own fluent retelling. The less confident should stick more closely to the original retelling; be wary of more confident children who may have a tendency to make the tale so elaborate that it loses impact.
- **Let pairs or individuals retell** – and ask the class to evaluate. In this way, children learn from each other.
- **Bit by bit** – with long stories, it can be helpful if children work on different sections of the story, bit by bit.
- **Perform** – when ready, ask the children to perform to other classes in pairs or individually; capture the performances on video or record on audio.
- **Writing** – finally, you may wish the children to move into writing. Use shared writing to show how the story may be crafted further as a precursor to the children's own writing.

Making the stories your own

Once the children have a fluent version of the basic story, then you can begin to craft the tale. This can be done in various ways, from the simple to the complex. For example:

- Substitutions – change a few details such as names, places, animals and objects. Basically, it is the same story but only a few words altered.
- Addition – retell the story, making a few changes but adding more details, description, events or dialogue. Try not to let it get out of control!
- Alteration – try altering characters or settings or events so that there are consequences. The story stays within the overall frame but may veer in new directions. Try changing the ending or altering the sequence of events.
- Change of view – retell from a different angle (by a different character or as a diary, letter or news report).
- Recycle the plot – retell, but alter everything except for the underlying plot pattern or theme.

Precede writing a new version by drawing a new story map or flowchart. Allow plenty of chances to retell the new story. Model how to do this with a new class version, then let the children draw their own new story and retell. They will need to retell their story at least three times for it to begin to become fluent. Some children will need at least six retellings before writing.

The Holy Man

About the story

This French story is in the tradition of many simple 'journey' or 'quest' stories in which one character sets off and on the way lots of others tag along. The story is both lively and enchanting – children adore retelling it. The idea of using other characters from different stories is an interesting one that young children would enjoy.

Getting to know the story well

Watch Xanthe Gresham's fantastic rendition of 'The Holy Man' on the CD-Rom and let the children enjoy joining in with the animal noises. Use some of the following activities to help the children get to know the story well.

Watch it
Watch this story being told by Xanthe Gresham on the CD-Rom.

Discuss

■ Ask the children: *Did all the animals really have a cough?* Establish the fact that some of the animals are pretending to be ill to allow them to join in the visit to the holy man. Why do the children think everyone's cough disappeared? (Because they no longer wanted to visit the holy man.)

■ Why do the children think the animals wanted to join in on the journey to visit the holy man?

Drama

■ It would be fun to act out this story with children in role as the animals. Encourage them to make a mini journey round the hall (or a space in the playground). The children will enjoy going to town with the animal noises. You could take on the role of the narrator.

Writing in role

■ As a piece of shared writing, invent a set of magical instructions for curing a cough. (It can make it easier if your ingredients are all from fairy tales.) For example:

> *First, walk to the end of a rainbow.*
> *Next, sip a cup of sunshine.*
> *After that, eat a golden apple.*
> *Finally, take a hair from a unicorn and place it under your pillow.*
> *This will cure a cough.*

Art

- Paint pictures of the animals all balanced on top of each other!

Dance and music

- As a class, practise the animal noises and see if you can make this rhythmic. Listen to Xanthe Gresham's version on the audio CD and imitate her rhythm. Encourage the children to add in actions as well.
- Invent a simple mime-dance to use when the animals make their noises.
- Add the noises and mime-dance to the retelling of the story as the children walk round the hall.

Retelling the story aloud

- In a relaxed environment, prepare the children to start telling the story themselves.
- Work on the bare bones of the story with the children and draw this as a story map (see example on page 6). The flowchart below shows how simple this could be.
- Using the story map or flowchart, work together on a short version of the story to tell.

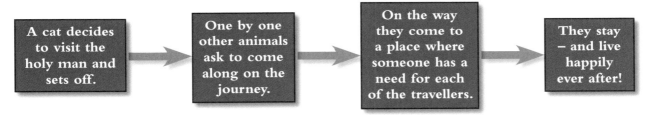

A cat decides to visit the holy man and sets off. → One by one other animals ask to come along on the journey. → On the way they come to a place where someone has a need for each of the travellers. → They stay – and live happily ever after!

From telling to writing

- When the children are confident in telling 'The Holy Man', challenge them to create their own version of the story.
- Start the children off by suggesting they use different animals in their version. When choosing animals they will have to think of creatures that the old lady, (or little old man perhaps) would need, so she can say, 'If only I had a dog to bark at strangers. If only I had a donkey to carry me to market…'
- Encourage the children to try rehearsing sentences that might prove useful for their own version. For instance, the opening sentence is a complex sentence with a relative clause. Try innovating orally, for example:

   Once upon a time there was a little black cat who had a cough.
   Once upon a time there was a little old dog who had a bad sneeze.
   Once upon a time there was a grey donkey who had a headache.

Why Dog Lives With Man

About the story

This story goes well alongside *The Cat's Drum* (on page 40 of *The Gingerbread Man and other stories*) because they are both simple myths explaining why the world is the way it is. Children love these simple explanatory tales which hinge around an early time when things were not as they are now. Many cultures have stories like these.

Getting to know the story well

As you watch Taffy Thomas tell this story on the CD-Rom (or tell it yourself), encourage the children to join in with the actions, the howling and the repeated phrases.

Watch it
Watch this story being told by Taffy Thomas on the CD-Rom.

Discuss

- Talk about the relationship between the animals. Why were the animals not able to be Dog's friend? Why was Man pleased to have Dog as a friend?
- It's quite easy to see why Man might be worried about Wolf and Bear, but can the children suggest why Man might be worried about Hare? (Perhaps Hare would eat his crops?)
- Discuss the nature of friendship. Ask the children to work in pairs to make lists of what friends do and how they behave towards each other.

Drama

- Once the children know the story well they can act as a storytelling chorus whilst others act out the tale. This would make a lovely assembly story.

Writing in role

- Write messages to different creatures asking to be their friend. Write replies.

Art

- Draw the creatures, showing how they increase in size.

Research

- Make lists of other animals that could be used instead of Hare, Wolf and Bear. They should ideally increase in size and be a threat to each other. For example, you could choose a mouse, a cat and a fox. The man would be afraid of the mouse because he might steal the corn, a cat might drink all the milk and the fox might kill the chickens!

Story behind the story

■ Retell the story from the point of view of Hare, Wolf or Bear. Start this by hot-seating the characters or interviewing them in role as journalists to find out what happened.

Retelling the story aloud

■ Prepare the children to start telling the story, or parts of the story, themselves. Watch or listen to Taffy Thomas tell the story again.

■ The short and repetitive nature of this tale makes it an excellent story for first-time storytellers to learn. Because Taffy Thomas has honed the story to the bare bones it can easily be learned word for word and performed for a choral retelling.

■ Use the following flowchart as a basis for drawing your story map.

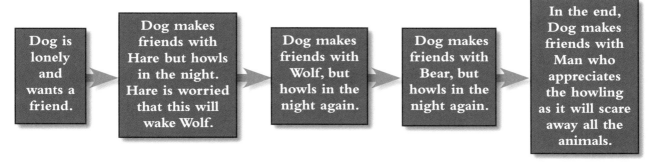

From telling to writing

■ You could retell this story as a simple substitution by just changing the animals over. This gives the sense of creating a new story but strongly relies on the original and is a good starting point for many children. You could swap the animals over but as Dog is known as 'man's best friend', you will probably have to stick with the dog. Remember, do not shift into the innovation until the original is known really well. So the beginning might be:

> *Once upon a time Dog lived on his own. But Dog got lonely. He thought he needed a friend.*
> *Dog spotted Rabbit. Dog thought that Rabbit could be his friend. Dog went over to Rabbit and said, "You and I could be friends."*
> *Rabbit said, "OK, we'll give it a go."*
> *In the daytime Dog and Rabbit went hunting together and at night they lay side by side. But in the middle of the night, Dog woke up and howled…*

■ Once the opening has been established, the children can add in more detail. For instance:

> *But in the middle of the night, Dog woke up. He just could not sleep. First he scratched. Then he rolled over. Still he could not sleep so he opened his mouth and HOWLED!!!*

The Gingerbread Man

About the story

In America this story is known as 'Johnny-Cake'. It is a very popular story that probably every infant knows. Taffy Thomas's version is a really good example of an innovation because he sets the story in his own locality and includes all sorts of local people that he knows.

Getting to know the story well

When telling the tale, start by hiding a gingerbread man in a tin and ask the children to guess what's inside the tin! Once you've watched or told the story, carry out some of the following activities to embed the key elements.

Discuss
- Talk about the sequence of events in the story. Ask: *Why did the gingerbread man run away? Why did everyone chase him? Do you think that everyone wants to eat the gingerbread man?*

Drama
- Hot-seat the characters of *The Gingerbread Man* and some of the animals or people who chase him.
- This is a lovely story to act out in the playground. Set out large apparatus to mark different places that the gingerbread man might visit. Children can play animals in role, wearing masks.

Writing in role
- Write a recipe for baking a gingerbread man – always made more interesting by adding some special 'magic' ingredient that is particular to your class.

Art
- Use a simple gingerbread man pattern for potato printing.

Research
- Look for other versions of the story. For instance, there is a very popular version which features a chapatti man rather than a gingerbread man.
- Find a map of Grasmere and use it to draw a map of the story, showing where the gingerbread man ran.

Story behind the story
- Retell the story from the fox's point of view.

Watch it
Watch this story being told by Taffy Thomas on the CD-Rom.

A baker bakes a gingerbread man.

It comes to life and runs away.

The baker chases it.

Other people keep joining in.

A fox helps the gingerbread man cross the river.

But eats it up instead!

Retelling the story aloud

- Below is a very simple version which younger children can learn communally and then use as a basis for their own retelling. The choral performance could be used as an assembly piece or in a 'storytelling festival' for other classes.
- In preparation for retelling, draw a story map (see example on page 6) for the story. The flowchart on the opposite page could be used for a basis.

Once upon a time there was Granny, who decided to make a gingerbread man. First she rolled out the gingerbread. Next she put in the eyes. Finally she popped the gingerbread man into the oven. Soon she could smell the gingerbread man cooking. Mmmmmmm!

As soon as she opened the oven door, the gingerbread man ran out of Granny's cottage!

"Stop, stop, little gingerbread man!" shouted Granny.

But the gingerbread man shouted, "Run, run as fast as you can, you can't catch me, I'm the gingerbread man."

So Granny followed the gingerbread man down the street till he came across a goat.

"Stop, stop, little gingerbread man!" bleated the goat.

But the gingerbread man shouted, "Run, run as fast as you can, you can't catch me, I'm the gingerbread man."

So Granny and the goat followed the gingerbread man down the lane till he came to a pig's sty.

"Stop, stop, little gingerbread man!" grunted the pig.

But the gingerbread man shouted, "Run, run as fast as you can, you can't catch me, I'm the gingerbread man."

So Granny, the goat and the pig followed the gingerbread man down the lane till he came to a river. Unfortunately, the gingerbread man could not swim.

However, Mr Fox was waiting by the river. "I'll take you across," shouted Mr Fox. "Jump on to my ears." So the gingerbread man jumped on to Mr Fox's ears. Mr Fox swam and he swam and he swam but the gingerbread man was getting wet. So he scrambled onto Mr Fox's nose and the fox ate him up – in – one – big – gulp!

From telling to writing

- Once the children can tell the simplified version of the story, watch Taffy Thomas's version and discuss how he has developed the telling. Now use his example to innovate on the story by adding in children from the class instead of animals. Set it in your own locality. If you take digital photos and make little cards with the children's faces then use Velcro, each day you can have different children in the story by sticking their faces onto the map at the relevant places.
- Explore varying the prepositions, for example *under* the hedge, *over* the field, *across* the road, *into* the fox's mouth!

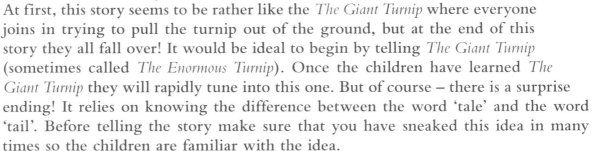

Farmer Merryweather's Cow

About the story

At first, this story seems to be rather like the *The Giant Turnip* where everyone joins in trying to pull the turnip out of the ground, but at the end of this story they all fall over! It would be ideal to begin by telling *The Giant Turnip* (sometimes called *The Enormous Turnip*). Once the children have learned *The Giant Turnip* they will rapidly tune into this one. But of course – there is a surprise ending! It relies on knowing the difference between the word 'tale' and the word 'tail'. Before telling the story make sure that you have sneaked this idea in many times so the children are familiar with the idea.

Getting to know the story well

Watch, read aloud or tell *Farmer Merryweather's Cow*. Use some of the following activities to help the children get to know the story well.

Watch it
Watch this story being told by Taffy Thomas on the CD-Rom.

Discuss

- Talk about the ending and what it might mean. Is the storyteller playing a trick on us? Did the story really happen?
- Discuss where milk comes from!

Drama

- Stories like this are fantastic for the smallest children to learn and act out as in the video of the story. When the children have learned the story communally, ask different children to take on the role of the characters in the story and to come out and try to pull the (imaginary!) cow out of the mud. This is a great story to act out for another class.

- Set out a farmyard area with model animals for the children to play at the story and make new ones up. This could be done in the sand area or by using suitable fuzzy felt shapes on a floor mat or model farm.

Writing in role

- Write a class thank-you letter from Farmer Merryweather to everyone who helped him try to pull his cow out of the mud.

Art

- Paint pictures of the cow and everyone pulling. Look at pictures of other farmyard animals that might get stuck in the mud and need rescuing.

Music and dance

- Sing 'The Farmer's in his Den' or 'Old Macdonald had a Farm' while moving to the rhythm of the music. Move the children into a circle and invite them to act out the animals, imitating the different animal noises. If you have children from other cultures it is interesting to hear the sounds animals make in different languages.

Research

- A farm trip would be ideal but if this is not possible, collect images or video clips of farm animals and the sounds they make.

Retelling the story aloud

- In a relaxed environment, once the children have heard the story at least three times, prepare them to start telling the story themselves.
- To prepare the children, use the structure of the flow chart below to create a story map (see example on page 6).
- Using the story map, learn the story as a class. Then put the children into groups. They could chant the story together or tell it sentence by sentence round the circle. Finally let them retell it in pairs.

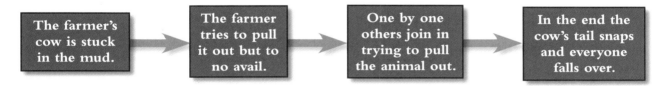

The farmer's cow is stuck in the mud. → The farmer tries to pull it out but to no avail. → One by one others join in trying to pull the animal out. → In the end the cow's tail snaps and everyone falls over.

From telling to writing

- When the children are confidently telling the story in their pairs, challenge them to create their own version of the story (either written or oral, depending on their skills).
- Like *The Gingerbread Man*, this story would be ideal for setting in the locality if your school is situated near the countryside. If not, then at least some of the children or adults in the school could become part of the story and help the farmer pull the animal out of the mud. Obviously, once the children have learned the pattern of the tale then they can keep adding more and more people in to help the farmer. Some young children just will not be able to understand the trick ending and they may want to change it so that the cow is rescued. For example:

    Suddenly, there was a loud pop!
        Everybody tumbled down on top of each other and Farmer Merryweather's cow came flying out of the mud. Everyone got up and cheered and Farmer Merryweather's cow gave the loudest moo of all!

The Cat's Drum

About the story

This story is a myth in the same tradition as *Why Dog Lives With Man*, as it explains how the cat began to purr. Use a little drum as you tell the story or, even better, a real cat to stroke so the children can hear it purring.

Getting to know the story well

Watch, read aloud or tell the story to the children.

Discuss

- This is a simple introduction to an animal myth (similar to *Why Dog Lives With Man*). Ask: *Do you think these myths are true?*
- Focus on the animals. Ask: *Why did the rat steal the drum? How did the cat feel about this? Why did the cat chase the rat?*

Dance and Music

- Provide simple music and ask the children to re-create cat and rat movements to the music. Add in drum beats to move to.

Retelling the story aloud

- Make sure that the children have listened to and joined in with the story a number of times before they attempt to tell the story in groups and then with a partner.
- To help their retelling, draw a story map so that they can see visually what happened. Create some actions to use.

From telling to writing

- When the children are confidently telling the story in their pairs, challenge them to create their own version. The sparse nature of the story leaves room for embellishment:

    Long ago, when the world began, the first pussycat owned a little drum. Every day the cat played on that drum. She loved the drum so much that she carried it everywhere that she went.
    One day a naughty rat stole the pussycat's drum. So the cat chased the rat. It chased the rat round and round and round…

- More confident children could write their own animal myth (perhaps how the dog got his bark or the cow her moo).

Watch it
Watch this story being told by Taffy Thomas on the CD-Rom.

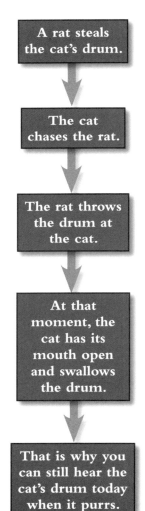

A rat steals the cat's drum.

The cat chases the rat.

The rat throws the drum at the cat.

At that moment, the cat has its mouth open and swallows the drum.

That is why you can still hear the cat's drum today when it purrs.

Greedy Fox

Getting to know the story well
Watch, read aloud or tell the story to the children.

Discuss
- Unpick the plot with the children. Ask: *Why did the fox put things into the bag? Why did everyone look inside the bag? Why are we intrigued by things we're told not to do?*
- Why did the dogs all chase the fox at the end? (The dogs' nature as much as our nature to be curious?)

Writing in role
- Write a newspaper article about what happened.

Art
- Organise the children to paint images showing the different scenes and put these on to the wall to show the story as a 'wall story'. Under the images put captions. Create a large wall map showing the journey that the fox takes.

Retelling the story aloud
- When the children have listened to and joined in with the story several times, ask them to tell the story with a partner.
- Prepare the children for telling by drawing a story map on the board, so that they can see visually what happened.
- The flowchart shows the key elements of the story.

From telling to writing

- This is a good story to innovate because the children can make simple changes to the tale. They could change what goes in the bag (for example, a bee which is eaten by a cockerel, which is chased by a pig which is chased off by a boy). You can change where he goes and whom he meets.

Watch it
Watch this story being told by Pie Corbett on the CD-Rom.

> Mr Fox sets out and puts a frog into his bag.

> He leaves the bag with a candlestick maker.

> The candlestick maker lets the frog out and it is eaten by a rat.

> The fox takes the rat, leaves it with a baker and gains a puppy.

> He leaves the puppy with a butcher and gains some meat.

> He is chased out of town by a pack of hounds.

The Little Red Hen

About the story

The story of *The Little Red Hen* has a wonderfully simple pattern and is an excellent story to be learned orally. You do have to watch that the children do not chant it so much that the rhythm takes over from the meaning. This story makes a very good first assembly for young children as everyone can chant it together and there are a few 'parts' to mime for those who feel confident.

Getting to know the story well

Read aloud or tell the story to the children. Use some of the following activities to help the children get to know the story well.

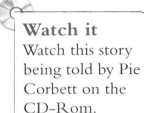

Watch it
Watch this story being told by Pie Corbett on the CD-Rom.

Discuss

■ Talk about all the different tasks that the little red hen had to do in the story. Ask questions such as: *Why did the animals not help the little red hen? Do you think they would have helped if they had been asked?*

■ Ask: *Why did the hen keep the bread at the end? Do you think that the hen should have shared the bread?*

■ What do the children think the moral of the story is?

Drama

■ Organise a hot-seat session with one child taking on the role of the little red hen. Four- and five-year-olds will want to know why she did not share the bread at the end and how she felt when the animals would not help.

■ Taking on the role of the narrator, practise a dramatised version of the tale with all the children taking on the part of an animal of their choice.

Writing in role

■ Ask the children to write simple messages from the other animals to the hen, saying 'sorry' for not helping her with her different tasks.

Art

■ Provide the children with paint and card and help them to create animal masks to use in a performance of the story.

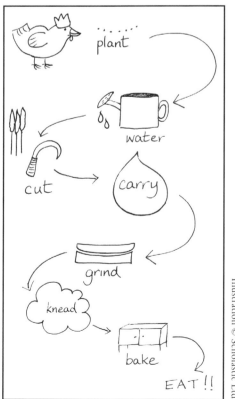

Dance

- Mime a simple dance to the rhythm of the story.

Music

- Sing 'Old Macdonald Had a Farm' or 'Chook, Chook, Chook, Good Morning Mrs Hen'. It would make a good opportunity to learn and act out the circle song 'The Farmer's in his Den'.

Research

- Organise a trip to a farm or research images of farms.
- A visit to a bakery to watch bread being made would add to the tale. Make bread so that the children experience kneading it.
- Bring in some wheat and give the children the opportunity to crush a few grains between a couple of stones to see how the grains begin to become flour.

Story behind the story

- Retell the story from the farmer's viewpoint, in role as the farmer. In preparation, read *Farmer Duck* by Martin Waddell.

Retelling the story aloud

- This is a great story to start oral story telling because the children will already be familiar with the story.
- On the video you can see the children joining in with the story, using actions. These can support both the events in a story but also be used to emphasise connectives such as 'once upon a time', 'early one morning', 'who'.
- Prepare the children for telling by drawing a story map on the board, so that the children can see visually what happened.

From telling to writing

- This makes an ideal story for shared writing. Ask the children to illustrate different parts of the text and create a class 'Big Book' or 'Wall Story'.
- To innovate, the children should keep the basic pattern and idea but just swap over the animals. So, cat might wake up and find the corn. She then asks help from other animals (such as a mouse, a dog, a donkey). Draw a new map with new animals and tell the 'new' story:

  Once upon a time there was a little white goose who lived on a farm. Early one morning he woke up and went outside. There he found some corn.
  "Who will help me plant the corn?" said the little white goose.
  "Not I," said the grey mouse.
  "Not I," said the old dog.
  "Not I," said the farmer's donkey…

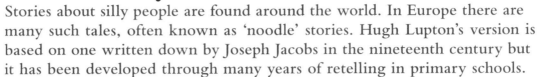

The Three Sillies

About the story

Stories about silly people are found around the world. In Europe there are many such tales, often known as 'noodle' stories. Hugh Lupton's version is based on one written down by Joseph Jacobs in the nineteenth century but it has been developed through many years of retelling in primary schools.

Getting to know the story well

Read aloud or tell the story to the children. Use some of the following activities to help the children get to know the story well.

Discuss

■ Focus on the silly people in the story. Who do the children think was the silliest and why? Enjoy the jokes with the children.

Drama

■ Role-play some of the scenes. Try retelling the story in the hall and encourage the children to run around acting out the tale as you tell it. This does not have to be formally organised in the sense of 'taking a part'. Just tell the story and allow the children to adopt a role to play as you tell it.

Art

■ Paint large moon pictures or use scrunched-up tissue paper to create a pinky-white moon.

■ Look at mirrors and puddles and discuss reflections.

■ Create simple fold-over patterns that show a reflection. Splodge paint on to a small piece of sugar paper. Fold this in half to create a pattern. Open up and see the image reflecting itself on either side.

Writing in role

■ Ask the children to write John's diary, putting in the three silly things that he saw. Model this in shared writing before the children write their own diary entries. It helps if you hot-seat John first so that the children have the chance to say the words before writing them.

■ Let the children practise hot-seating in pairs, with one child as John and the other as the interviewer. Encourage them to swap roles so both have a chance to say what happened.

Music

■ Sing 'Nick, Nack, Paddywhack' which is a silly song about a silly person.

Research

■ Find other 'noodle' stories about silly people. It might also be a good excuse to tell jokes. Though many young children are not too sure what a joke is, it is fun to hold joke-telling sessions. The ability to understand a joke is generally a good indicator of linguistic sophistication.

Retelling the story aloud

- In a relaxed environment, prepare the children to start telling the story themselves.
- This story is really an excuse to tell three noodle stories. They are stories set within one story which acts as a frame. Organise the children to tell the story in groups of four, with one child telling the beginning and end of the story and one child telling each of the three silly stories.
- Prepare the children for telling by drawing a story map on the board, so that the children can see visually what happened.
- The flowchart shows the key elements of the story.
- The children could each learn one of the stories and work in groups of three to present the whole tale.

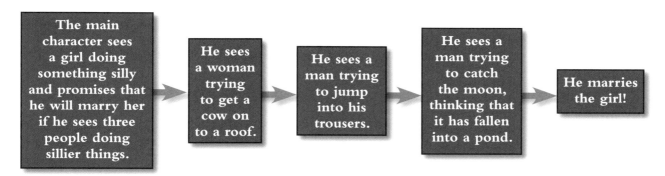

The main character sees a girl doing something silly and promises that he will marry her if he sees three people doing sillier things. → He sees a woman trying to get a cow on to a roof. → He sees a man trying to jump into his trousers. → He sees a man trying to catch the moon, thinking that it has fallen into a pond. → He marries the girl!

From telling to writing

- When the children are confidently telling the story in their pairs, challenge them to create their own version of the story.
- It might be fun just to take the three silly people and write each of their stories. Ask the children to choose their favourite story out of the three and tell and then write it from the point of view of the silly person. For example:

Once upon a time there was a little old lady who lived in a little old cottage. Her cottage was so old that the straw on the roof had begun to rot and grass was growing there instead.

Early one morning, the little old lady went out to fetch her cow Daisy from the meadow. Unfortunately, there was not much grass left in the meadow. Now the little old lady had an idea because there was plenty of grass on the roof of her little old cottage.

So she led her cow back home…

The Fox and the Stork

About the story

Everyone knows some of Aesop's fables, the most common being *The Hare and the Tortoise* which appears in many cultures – often with other animals. The distinct point about a fable is that there is a lesson to be learned. Fables are usually, though not exclusively, about animals who behave like humans.

    The tale hinges around the notion that the stork could not eat from the flat plate and the fox could not eat from the tall glasses, so the children need to know what the two animals look like.

Getting to know the story well

Display images of foxes and storks for the class before you tell the story. Read aloud or tell the story to the children. Use some of the following activities to help the children get to know the story well.

Discuss

- Unpick the central problem of the story with the children. Ensure that they understand why Stork could not eat and why Fox could not eat. Bring in containers of different shapes to show the problem for Stork and Fox.
- Ask: *What is the story telling us – what is the 'moral'?*

Drama

- Set up an area that is either Fox or Stork's home – with a little table and tea things for the children to use as a role-play area in pairs. Ask the children to role-play the two tea parties.

Writing in role

- Write letters between Fox and Stork, perhaps apologising for their behaviour.
- Ask the children to make a list of animals to invite to a party. Tell them to design and write invitations.
- In a shared writing session, write a poem about who you would not invite to the party and why. For example:

  I won't invite bee
  Because of her buzz.
  I won't invite crocodile
  In case she snaps.
  I won't invite tortoise
  Because he is too slow…

Art

- Collect images of foxes and storks and use these to make a class collage.

Research

- Use books and the internet to research other Aesop fables.
- Set the children to research what food storks and foxes actually eat.

Retelling the story aloud

- In a relaxed environment, prepare the children to start telling the story themselves.
- Prepare the children for telling by drawing a story map on the board, so that they can see visually what happened. Ask them to draw their own versions of the story map and to use these to retell the story in pairs.
- The flowchart below shows the key elements of the story:

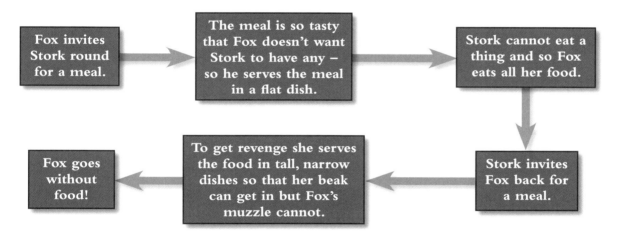

From telling to writing

- Hot-seat both characters and get them to tell the story from their different viewpoints, in the first person. Use this as a basis for writing, with half the class as storks and half in role as foxes. For example:

Last week Foxy asked me round for a meal. When I arrived there was a delicious smell. He invited me straight in and sat me down at his table. You can imagine how sad I felt when I saw the dishes. They were all flat and I knew that I would not be able to eat a thing. I tried but my beak just couldn't pick up anything. Foxy was watching me all the time with his beady eyes and I'm sure that he did it on purpose....

Monkey and Turtle

> **About the story**
> This story comes from Java, Indonesia.

Getting to know the story well
Use some of the following activities to help the children get to know the story well.

Discuss
- Talk about why Monkey and Turtle might want clothes. Ask: *Why did they never manage to make them? How do you think they felt about each other? Why did they set each other different jobs?*
- There is a simple lesson to be learned from the story: that some things never change. Can the children think of other examples of how some things never change?

Drama
- Ask the children to role-play the conversations between Monkey and Turtle. Contrast how they behave at night and in the day.
- Discuss and mime how we behave on chilly and hot days.

Art
- Find representations of creatures in Javanese art. Use these as the basis for art work. Make turtle and monkey masks.

Retelling the story aloud
- This is a good story for children to tell in pairs, with each child taking the part of a different animal.
- To help the children in their retelling, draw a story map on the board and create some actions to use with the story.

From telling to writing

- Challenge the children to create their own story using different contrasting animals (for example, a spider and a giraffe).
- Demonstrate with Year 2 children how to turn their spoken words into written dialogue. Add adverbs or extend the speech, showing what the speaker is doing: *"Brrr! Brother!" chattered Monkey icily, shaking his head as he spoke."*

At night it is very cold.

Monkey and Turtle decide to make clothes to keep warm like man.

Monkey suggests jobs for Turtle – which will keep him warm.

Turtle suggests jobs for Monkey – which will keep him warm.

When it is daytime, it is sunny so they do nothing!

At night the cold returns and so they set to discussing making clothes... and so it goes on until this day!

The Udala Tree

About the story

This story comes from Nigeria. It is a magical story in which a girl who is downtrodden finds some magic and becomes powerful. It is a great one to tell because of the rhythmic refrain. On the audio recording, I tried to give it a singsong rhythm but you may prefer to do a percussive chant – or sing it aloud.

Getting to know the story well

Use some of the following activities to help the children get to know the story well.

Discuss

■ Discuss the sequence of events. Ask: *Can you think of another story in which a girl character has to work hard while others sit around?*

Drama

■ Have a hot-seat session with a child taking the role of Sia Jetta and others the brothers. Encourage the rest to give Sia Jetta advice.

Music

■ Use a range of percussion instruments to create background music to accompany the chanting in the story.

Retelling the story

■ When the children have listened to and joined in with the story a number of times, they can attempt to tell the story to a partner.
■ Prepare the children for telling by drawing a story map.

From telling to writing

■ Reset the tale in another location, using the same pattern:

Once upon a time there was a little boy called Abdul who did all the work. He swept the floors, he washed the dishes. He kept the windows shiny and went to the market. All the while, his sisters did nothing except sit around dozing in the sun.

One day Abdul was walking back from the shops when he found a tiny, golden seed. He knew it was special so he hid the seed under his pillow. That night he had an amazing dream. In his dream he saw the golden seed growing into...

> Sia Jetta works whilst her brothers laze.

> She finds a seed which grows into a tree bearing fruit.

> She warns her brothers not to climb the tree but they disobey her.

> She punishes them by making the tree grow into the clouds.

> They promise to mend their ways.

> She saves them and they keep their promise.

Ananse and the Golden Box of Stories

About the story

There are many versions of this story, both in Africa and the Caribbean, in which Ananse finds or keeps all the stories of the world. Ananse is a trickster so is often shown as being very clever. The story uses the idea of a character being set a number of 'tests' or 'challenges'. The idea of a doll covered in a sticky substance is often used for capturing someone. Boxes also often feature in tales, such as the one that Pandora opened.

Getting to know the story well

Watch, read aloud or tell the story to the children. Use some of the following activities to help the children get to know the story.

Watch it
Watch this story being told by Jane Grell on the CD-Rom.

Discuss

- Talk about the sequence of events in this story. Why did Ananse want the box of stories? As a class, discuss the different reasons why people like stories.
- How many places can the children think of where they might hear stories? (For example: at home, tucked up in bed; at the library, at school.)
- Ask: *Do you think Nyame expected Ananse to meet the challenge he set? Why do you think he set such a difficult challenge?*

Drama

- Divide the class into pairs and ask the children to role-play the initial meeting between Nyame and Ananse. Encourage the children to think carefully about how each character would act towards the other. (Nyame is a great god who commands respect, while Ananse is a little spiderman.)
- Encourage the children to act out the three scenes where Ananse traps the Osebo, Mboro and Moatia.
- Ask the children to role-play the final meeting between Ananse and Osebo. What has changed? Would Nyame act differently towards Ananse?

Writing in role

- Ask the children to write instructions for: 'How to capture Osebo, the leopard of the terrible teeth', 'How to trap Mboro, the hornets who sting like fire' or 'How to catch Moatia, the fairy who is never seen'.

- In preparation for another activity (see 'From telling to writing'), discuss and invent other ways of trapping different animals that might be used in your own story version.

Art

- Hornets make an interesting shape to draw. Provide a selection of pictures for reference and ask the children to draw a hornet. Enlarge the pictures considerably in order to create an effective display.
- Model hornets could also be made out of wire and papier-mâché.

Research

- Read other Ananse stories. Children of African or Caribbean heritage may have relatives who can pass on some stories.

Story behind the story

- Tell the story of how the golden box came to fly open. Tell one of the stories that flew out of the box.

Retelling the story aloud

- Prepare the children for telling by drawing a story map on the board, so that they can see visually what happened. Ask them to draw their own versions of the story map and to use these to retell the story in pairs.
- Once they are fluently retelling the original, work together to create a new map and version.
- Allow sufficient time for the children to retell the story in their pairs, refining their tellings.

Someone has all the stories of the world in a box.

↓

Ananse wants all the stories and is set three tasks to achieve in return for the stories.

↓

Ananse achieves each task which involves trapping a creature by trickery.

↓

The box of stories is given as a reward to Ananse.

↓

Unfortunately, the box opens and all the stories escape.

From telling to writing

- This would be a good story to retell with a few minor changes or embellishments. Looking at other versions will also help to generate different possibilities.
- Discuss ideas for who Ananse might be asked to trap – and most importantly what tricks could be used to trap the animals. Once you have decided on those details, then it is easy enough to drop them in to create a new story. For example:

> So Ananse crept down to the pool, three in his net and waited. After some time, Tiger came passing by and asked Ananse what he was doing.
> "I am looking for my golden plate which I was washing in the water and have dropped," said Ananse.
> Now, Tiger was always greedy for gold so he too began to peer into the water. Immediately, Ananse crept behind tiger and pushed him into the water, into the large fishing net. Within a few seconds, he had trapped Tiger.

The Door in the Mountain

About the story

This is a lovely story from Wales. Lots of small children want to have adventures away from home but need to know that they can always get back again. The story uses the idea of a doorway into another world inhabited by friendly little people who always should be obeyed. Unfortunately, Betsi is tempted and forgets what she has been warned. Of course, she manages to escape in the end.

Getting to know the story well

Use some of the following activities to help the children get to know the story.

Discuss

■ Talk about the sequence of events. How is the story similar to *The Lion, the Witch and the Wardrobe* or *Stargate*?

Writing in role

■ Write a letter from Betsi to the little people, apologising for having picked the daffodil.

Art

■ As a class, make a large-scale painting of a mountain and cut out a door that can be opened. Paint the lake and boat inside.
■ Bring in a bunch of daffodils for the children to paint.

Story behind the story

■ Tell the story of another person who finds the same doorway.

Retelling the story aloud

■ Draw a story map so that the children can see visually what happened before attempting to tell the story with a partner.

Betsi finds a doorway into the world of the little people.

She explores the other world.

She is warned by little people not to pick any flowers.

Betsi picks a daffodil and has to flee.

She escapes home with the daffodil.

She cannot find the doorway ever again.

From telling to writing

■ In a shared writing session, let a character go through a different gateway, have a mini adventure and then find their way back in the nick of time. For example:

> *Zoe paused and stared. There was a small doorway in the bank at the side of the road. She had never noticed it before. Now she knew that she shouldn't but curiosity had always been her second name, so Zoe turned the handle and opened it...*

Tommy and the Elves

About the story

Jess Smith is a traveller storyteller. *Tommy and the Elves* is another good example of what happens if you try to cross the little folk – in this case, an elf! It includes a classic riddling contest which is found in many other great tales.

Getting to know the story well

Write some riddles. Begin by thinking of something such as a clock. Then make a list of clues such as: it tells time, its hands move, it is a circle shape. Now use the clues to make a simple riddle – for example: *I tell the time, wave my hands and am the same shape as the moon. What am I?*

Art
■ Ask the children to paint, draw or make play dough models of the elves with their green hats and pointed toe-boots.

Research
■ Collect other riddles to display. Pretend that an elf has visited the class. Hide a tiny elf letter for the children to find and reply to.

Story behind the story
■ Tell the story of the nasty elf and how he came to think that he owned the river.

Retelling the story aloud
■ Make sure the children have listened to and joined in with the story a number of times before they attempt to retell the story to a partner.
■ The flowchart (see right) shows the key elements of the story.

> The main character is about to do something when an elf appears.

> The elf sets three riddles.

> The main character finds help.

> The riddles or tasks are accomplished.

> The main character is able to do or gets whatever was wanted in the beginning.

From telling to writing

■ This is a lovely story to innovate. The children could just retell the same story with a few simple changes. For instance, they might decide to build up the setting. What can they see? What can they hear? For example:

> *It was a sunny morning when Tommy went for a walk down by the river. The water shimmered in the sunlight. Green rushes grew at the edge. He could see a white swan gliding under the bridge which curved over the river like an arch.*

Monkey See, Monkey Do!

About the story
This story probably comes from India. It is an ideal one for young children to retell. You need a bag or box full of hats – of every shape, size and colour!

Getting to know the story well
Use some of the following activities to help the children become familiar with the story.

Watch it
Watch this story being told by Pie Corbett on the CD-Rom.

Discuss
- Talk about the events in the story. Why did the monkeys copy? What happened at the end? Why did the hat seller throw his hat down? Did he know what the monkeys would do?

Art
- Create a jungle area with hanging vines. Paint or print animal patterns, or make masks for the monkeys to wear.
- Challenge the children to design and make simple hats.

Dance
- Create a monkey dance with the children working in pairs, imitating each other in time to music.

Story behind the story
- Retell the story in role as a monkey storyteller from the point of view of the monkeys.

Retelling the story aloud
- This is a short enough story for the children to attempt to learn to tell themselves. Make sure you have a large box full of hats.

From telling to writing

- For an innovation the story has to be nearly the same – though you may want to add in more detail. For example:

  Once upon a time there was a poor hat seller. All his life he had worked hard, saving money till in the end he had a fine selection of hats for sale. Early one frosty morning, he set out for the nearby town. Now on his way he had to pass through a forest…

A hat seller's cart falls over, spilling out all the hats.

↓

Monkeys steal all the hats.

↓

Whatever the hat seller does to get the hats back, the monkeys copy him.

↓

In the end he gives up – and as a final gesture of irritation he throws his own hat on to the ground.

↓

And of course, all the monkeys do the same – so he gets his hats back!

The Golden Goose

About the story

The Golden Goose is a well-known European tale. It is another story in which someone is on a journey and everyone tags along, but in this case the people have no option because they get stuck to the golden goose.

Whilst the idea that a girl's hand in marriage can be granted so easily by her father might sit awkwardly with today's values, the idea that a person who makes someone else happy and might make a good companion in a relationship is a useful message.

Getting to know the story well

Read aloud or tell the story to the children. Use some of the following activities to embed the story.

Discuss

- Talk about the events described in the story. Ask: *Why didn't anyone realise that they would get stuck to the goose? What made the Princess laugh? Why did Jack want to take the goose to the King? Was it his intention to make the Princess laugh?*

Drama

- This is a story that begs to be acted out, possibly the first time that you tell it. Use the hall and get everyone coming out to hold on to each other so you make a huge train of people.
- Ask the children to imagine some of the ways in which people tried to make the Princess laugh. Do they think they succeeded? Set up a hot-seat session, with one child in role as the princess and other class members trying to make her laugh. You will need to choose a princess who can keep a straight face!

Writing in role

- As a class, write a newspaper report about what happened. Some of the children could be news reporters.

Art

- Collect feathers to make a collage version of the golden goose. Feathers are available from craft suppliers but you may also get some from a visit to a local farm or wildlife sanctuary. Gold paint spray can be used to transform the feathers.

Dance and Music

- Create simple percussive rhythms for the journey. Use three chime bars to invent a tune. Invent a chorus for everyone to sing with more and more voices, such as:

  'Turn us loose, turn us loose,
  We're all stuck to the golden goose!'

Research

■ Find out more about geese and show the children some pictures.

■ Try to find some other stories that feature geese (for example, *The Goose Girl*).

Story behind the story

■ Tell the Princess's story. What really happened that made her so sad?

Retelling the story aloud

■ After sharing the story many times, prepare the children for telling by drawing a story map on the board so that they can see visually what happened.

■ Ask the children to draw their own versions of the story map and to use these to retell the story in pairs.

■ The flowchart (see right) shows the key elements of the story.

■ Use story circles where each child says the next sentence.

■ Move on to retelling in pairs, where the children pass the story back and forth.

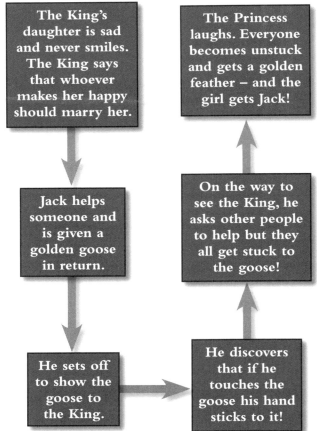

From telling to writing

■ When the children are confidently telling the story in their pairs, challenge them to create their own story. As this is another story with a journey that involves lots of characters, this could be innovated by resetting it in the local area and peopled by children or local characters. For example:

The first place he came to was the primary school where he saw Mrs Jenkins on playground duty. 'What a beautiful goose,' said Mrs Jenkins, reaching out to stroke the goose. Unfortunately, as soon as she touched the goose, her hand became stuck fast and she just could not let go! So Mrs Jenkins called out to the headteacher for help...

■ Of course, you could change the animal from a goose to something else with magical properties. You may want to alter the idea of the girl having to marry whoever cheers her up as well. Remember that the values within a story are a reflection of the time when they were told – and many traditional tales hold values that we might not subscribe to nowadays. Perhaps the children can think of a more fitting reward!

Michael Barry

TALES OF THE PERMANENT WAY
Stories from the Heart of Ireland's Railways

Andalus Press

Published by Andalus Press
7 Frankfort Avenue, Dublin 6
Ireland
www.andalus.ie
info@andalus.ie

By the same author:
Across Deep Waters, Bridges of Ireland
Restoring a Victorian House
Through the Cities, the Revolution in Light Rail
Homage to al-Andalus, the Rise and Fall of Islamic Spain

Jacket
Front cover: photograph, courtesy Ulster Folk & Transport Museum;
'Princess' watercolour, courtesy of Debra Wenlock.
Back cover: photograph, Michael Barry.
Back flap: author photograph, Veronica Barry

Jacket design by Anú Design.
Book design by Michael Barry.

Printed by Printer Trento S.r.l. Italy.

ISBN 978-0-9560383-1-9

Contents

For Michael Daniel Barry

Acknowledgements

Producing a book is a solitary experience. One is thus very grateful when people demonstrate their kindness on being asked for assistance. My sincere thanks are due to the following: firstly, Eileen Kelly, Chief Civil Engineer, Iarnród Éireann, for support and encouragement to produce a book in this, the 175th anniversary of the railways in Ireland. My colleagues in Iarnród Éireann proved extraordinarly helpful. These include: Vincent Brady, Dan Murray, Stephen Hirsch, Kieran O' Donnell, Ken Wade, Tony Bambrick, Michael Kiernan, Bernard Coleman, Michael Danaher, Jim Shaw, Liam Meagher, Paddy Quinn, Jim Donovan, Derek Whelan, Liam Conmy, Frank Golden, Kathy Kissane, John Mullin, Jack Ryan, Seán Maxwell, Gerry Healy, John O' Mahony, Conor Murphy, Tom Heffernan, Joanne Bisset, Barry Kenny, Paddy Mangan, Gregg Ryan, Tara O' Rourke, Joe Walsh and Ronan Gill. Nick West kindly lent me memorabilia that belonged to his grandfather, Arthur Plumer, and this allowed me to give additional historical depth to the book. Oliver Doyle gave me useful historical information, as did Eugene Fox. Noel Armstrong assisted in introducing me to a wide number of interviewees in the west. Kevin Forde guided me though the IÉ/CIÉ photo archives, consisting of mostly photographs taken by himself and Paddy Scully. I am grateful for the help given me by Tom Grimes, Ciara Quinn and Kevin Fitzpatrick of CIÉ.

Mark Kennedy, Railway Curator, Ulster Folk & Transport Museum, could not have been more helpful with advice and provision of photographs. He also showed me the railway exhibits, including the extensive collection of permanent way artefacts that are kept on the Cultra campus. Debra Wenlock, artist, kindly allowed me to use her marvellous illustration of the 'Princess' locomotive. The members of the Irish Railway Record Society (IRRS) have as usual, been extremely kind. In particular, I would like to mention Clifton Flewitt and the archivist, Brendan Pender, for access to the archive and library at their HQ in Heuston. Joe St. Leger in Cork, stalwart photographer of the railway, and particularly, permanent way activities, kindly lent me some photos. Derek Paine, assiduous recorder of the history of Greystones and beyond, lent me unique historical photos of Bray Head. Sandra McDermott of the National Library of Ireland was kind enough to allow me to use images from the O' Dea Collection. The Permanent Way Institution was supportive, with particular thanks to Martin Fairbrother and Colin Cowey. Mary Molloy of the Railway Safety Commission gave me useful advice. Andrew McGivern, District Engineer, Translink, was very helpful in giving me Northern Ireland Railways (NIR) contacts. Elaine McCurdy, of NIR, kindly sent me photos. Louise Lawler, Archivist, Bord na Móna, gave me information and photographs about the extensive rail network that they operate.

Of course, this book would not be possible without the generosity of my interviewees, who granted me the time and also put up with my attempts to capture a portrait. They are: Harold Mc Intyre, J. J. Maxwell, Tom O' Donnell, Denis Redmond, Peter Mc Morrough, Jim Cregan, Dan Donovan, Michael Keane, Vincent Moran, Liam Brennan, Neilus O' Donoghue, Pat Jennings, Eddie Connor, Bob Fahey, Tony Marshall, Michael Baneham, Brian Garvey, Denis Grimshaw, Michael Browne, Michael Flynn, Mike Devaney, Josie Ferguson, Noel Armstrong, Kevin O' Connor, Tom Grady, Tom Spellman, Steven Gaughran, Brian Lucas, Brendan Mc Cormack, Pat Mc Carthy, Vernon Kiely, John O' Brien, Pat Higgins, Niall Lynch and Huda Yousif. Interviews took place in the period October 2008 to July 2009. I wish to acknowledge the kindness of two interviewees, both of whom I was privileged to meet in October 2008: Paddy Hunt, who died in January 2009, and Tom Young, who died in May 2009.

Daltún Ó Ceallaigh kindly read my words. He advised me on grammatical matters, as did Angela Plunkett. Jim and Phyl Casey advised, as did Dermot O' Doherty. Veronica Barry once more patiently edited and afforded me the time and space to write this book.

The Permanent Way

'On the ballast is the permanent way, which consists of sleepers, fastenings, rails, fish plates, points, crossings and all the materials which form the road on which the railway vehicles run. The expression 'permanent way' is employed to distinguish the materials of the finished railway from the materials of the temporary tram-roads used by contractors during the construction of the line.'

Text Book of Science, Railway Appliances, 1878.

Foreword

Sunday evening on the track in the early 1980s, to the south of Sandycove Station, near Dublin, during the DART construction project, at the end of a long day's work: it was time to join up the track and get it open for traffic. The men were gathered around the permanent way inspector at the centre who was kneeling down making the final arrangements. This scene has been repeated innumerable times, the permanent way inspector taking the step of putting the line back, ready for trains – a task of great responsibility. Trains could now run at line speed along this track. I was privileged to be there then and on many similar occasions. I have been fortunate to be part of the permanent way family in Ireland and can sincerely say that, in my career, I have not met a more dedicated and responsible group of people.

So why this book? Over the years I heard the tales of the work that these men carried out, in all conditions and weathers. This work, by its nature, is in the background, spread throughout the Irish railway network. The travelling public in Ireland rarely sees the permanent way staff who work diligently, ensuring that the railway tracks are safe and open for the trains that they take. I eventually decided to record some of the stories before they were lost, from both serving and retired permanent way people. This book is not a technical tome; rather it has the intention of telling, in an accessible way, the fascinating story of the people who maintain Ireland's railway lines.

It is a long and honourable tradition. People have been maintaining the track on the railways in Ireland for 175 years. When the railways first came to Ireland, it was the advanced technology of the time. The network spread rapidly around the country. By 1860 most of the main cities and towns had a railway connection. The employees (station staff, signalmen, engine drivers and permanent way staff), all over the country, were an elite of sorts. The railway provided good steady employment. It meant that this advanced technology and organisation of the time extended throughout what was then an agricultural society. From then onwards the roots of the railway family in Ireland were laid down. Most Irish people are likely to have, in their ancestry, connections to someone who worked on the railway, with a fair chance that it might have been in the permanent way.

The whole ethos of a railway is that the train is assured of a clear route, that it can travel down the track at speed, on the basis that the track is safe and that the line is fenced off, separated from possible obstructions. The essential point is that the train is king of its own domain, which is the permanent way and the bridges and tunnels associated with it. Our permanent way workers have to work continually to ensure that this is indeed so.

The travelling public, when they stand on a station platform and look at the track, if they pay any attention to it at all, might think that this is an eternal fixture. Strong substantial rails, solid sleepers, sitting in their bed of ballast – surely it is an inert medium, not needing much attention? However, the track is a dynamic medium. Sleepers and fastenings deteriorate after years of pounding. Ballast gets dirty and can settle. The rails need attention. Flooding occurs. For this, and a myriad of other reasons, the track must be carefully maintained.

When the track wears out, as it does within 30 years, it must be renewed. Most of this work is done at off-peak times, and increasingly at night, so as not to disrupt the travelling public.

While the system has become increasingly mechanised, it still involves heavy physical work for a permanent way worker. Technology has helped in the eternal vigilance that is given to the track: rails are tested by ultrasonic probes as well as by a high technology track recording vehicle, which travels the network. However, despite this technology, the human eye is still needed. Permanent way men patrol Ireland's railway tracks at least once a week. There is and always has been a high degree of professionalism in what is a very responsible job. It must be remembered that they do not work in isolation – they also work closely with the other departments of the railway, which give stalwart service. They are part of the wider family such as the Operators and the Mechanical and Signal Engineers, all working together towards delivering the finished product, that is, the operation of the passenger and freight train services.

For this book, I cast my net to include not just the track but also the other things that maintaining the permanent way entails, including the bridges and tunnels. The photographs and illustrations that I gathered endeavour to illustrate the story from the earliest days of primitive track and rudimentary steam locomotives and carriages, through to the modern permanent way and machinery that help provide a path for today's sophisticated trains that run at 160 kph.

The history of the Irish permanent way is proud and distinguished. It is also worth remembering its innovative and international dimension. The flat-bottom, or 'Vignoles', rail was developed by that eponymous engineer, born in Wexford. The 1,600 mm track gauge was first used in Ireland and railways in Australia and Brazil followed. The Bretland Tracklayer, advanced technology developed in 1920s Mullingar, was copied in Britain and, most likely, in the Soviet Union. In the 1990s and onwards Irish permanent way experts gave consultancy advice to railways across, inter alia, Eastern Europe, the former Soviet Union, Africa and Asia.

The book is structured to include an introductory history (Chapter 1) in order to give context to the stories that follow. (Refer to the glossary at the back for an explanation of railway terms.) The stories in the book show the human face of working at the heart of the Irish railways. The stories are, in part, serious and, in many parts humorous. The reason the work got done, even in hard times, was partly because of the humour and camaraderie that the permanent way men generated. I have been privileged to be able to reproduce in Chapter 2 an account written by the late Arthur M. Plumer, an engineer whose experience dated back to the railway during the Civil War era and continued up to the mid-20th century. His story represents the start of the transition to the modern railway. That transition continues in the stories (set out in Chapters 3 and 4) that I garnered when I travelled round the country talking to the men, and now women, of the permanent way, both retired and still working for the railway, as the case may be. This is their story, in their words.

Michael Barry
Dublin, July 2009

Chapter 1
The Permanent Way Emerges

The invention of the railway was one of the great discoveries of the 19th century. It soon became one of the essential foundations on which Victorian prosperity was built. The railways spread rapidly. As they developed, increasingly heavier and faster steam locomotives were introduced. The track evolved, in turn, and eventually came to form the types of rail and tranverse sleepers that we see today.

The concept of rail as a means of transportation goes back many centuries. Mining and quarrying was an area which required heavy loads to be moved in an efficient manner. However, wagons and carts got bogged down on the rough mine tracks. As ever, man's ingenuity came to the fore. The practice of laying down timber beams was adopted to offer an easier surface along which the cart could be propelled, whether by man or animal power. These came to be known as wagon ways or tramways and were used in mines in Europe from the 16th century. But a drawback with timber wheels and timber beams was rapid wear of both. Records from the early 1700s show that iron plating was laid over the timber to minimise wear. Incidentally the term for a permanent way worker, 'platelayer', derives from this era. In addition, iron wheels were introduced. A horse could haul a larger load with iron wheels on some form of iron guideway. As the Industrial Revolution took hold during the second half of the 18th century, there occurred the momentous invention of the steam engine. The concept of a mobile steam engine reached fruition with Richard Trevithick's development of a steam locomotive, which first operated at Coalbrookdale in Shropshire in 1802. The Stockton & Darlington Railway, which opened in 1825, used steam locomotives to haul goods trains. The Liverpool & Manchester Railway opened five years later and transported passengers and goods. Thus the railway age began. 'Projectors' developed schemes, surveyed the land and began to build railways across Britain and, in due course, continental Europe.

The railway age came early to Ireland. The genesis of the project occurred after the development of Dunleary Harbour, which commenced in 1817 under the eminent Scottish engineer John Rennie. Dunleary was renamed Kingstown in consequence of King George IV's departure from its new harbour after his 1821 Irish visit. The silting up of Dublin Port gave impetus to the idea of running a ship-canal from the city to connect with the new harbour. However, the canal project never progressed. The accelerating railway developments across the water inspired promoters to arrive at the concept of a railway and the Dublin & Kingstown Railway Act received Royal Assent in September 1831.

The initial plan for the line had been prepared by another eminent Scottish engineer, Alexander Nimmo, builder of an impressive range of roads, bridges and harbours in Connemara, but he died in 1832. Charles Blacker Vignoles, a native of Wexford and with experience of the early railway projects in England, was subsequently appointed Chief Engineer. The building of a railway commenced in April 1833. The route was from a terminus at Westland Row in Dublin to Kingstown, terminating at the western end of the Old Harbour. The contracted length was 'five miles, 43 chains and four yards'. Much of the line ran along the coast. The contractor selected for the works was William Dargan, now regarded as the father of the Irish railways. Experienced in building roads and canals, he was to play a prominent part in the construction of the Irish railways in the great expansion that followed.

Above right. The first rails were used in mines. Here is seen a 16th century miner's cart with wooden wheels on timber logs. (Transport Museum, Berlin)

Right. 'Fish-bellied' cast iron rail used at Arigna, Co. Roscommon, where iron ore was smelted using local coal. Here, from the early part of the 19th century, haulage was by horse-drawn carts which ran on rails. (Ulster Folk & Transport Museum)

Right. A view of the opening of the Stockton & Darlington Railway in 1825. (Ulster Folk & Transport Museum)

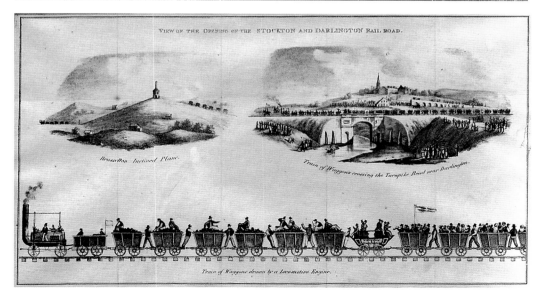

VIEW OF THE OPENING OF THE STOCKTON AND DARLINGTON RAIL ROAD.

Brusselton Inclined Plane.

Train of Waggons crossing the Turnpike Road near Darlington.

Train of Waggons drawn by a Loco-motive Engine.

Tools used in construction were primitive, principally barrows, picks and shovels. Bridges and tunnels were erected. Granite came from quarries at Dalkey and Seapoint. Large amounts of filling were placed and great sea embankments were constructed, some with a parabolic shape, all the better to repel the waves. Eventually, on 17th December 1834, the railway was opened and the locomotive Hibernia hauled around 5,000 passengers between Dublin and Kingstown in the course of the day. This was the world's first suburban railway.

The track gauge, or distance between the inside faces of the running rails, was built to 4 ft 8 ½ in (1,435 mm). This was in common use in England at the time and, as the initial locomotive and carriages were manufactured there, it was a pragmatic solution. The track consisted of rails spanning two granite blocks of about 680 mm square and 300 mm deep. The blocks were spaced at 900 mm centres, and were set on a bed of shingle taken from such as Killiney beach. The rails, sitting on a felt pad, were wedged in cast iron chairs. The chairs were fixed to the granite blocks by pins driven in oak plugs. The rails were rolled in 15 foot lengths and weighed 45 lb per yard and were a form of wrought iron. K. A. Murray, in his book *Ireland's First Railway*, relates the specification for the rails

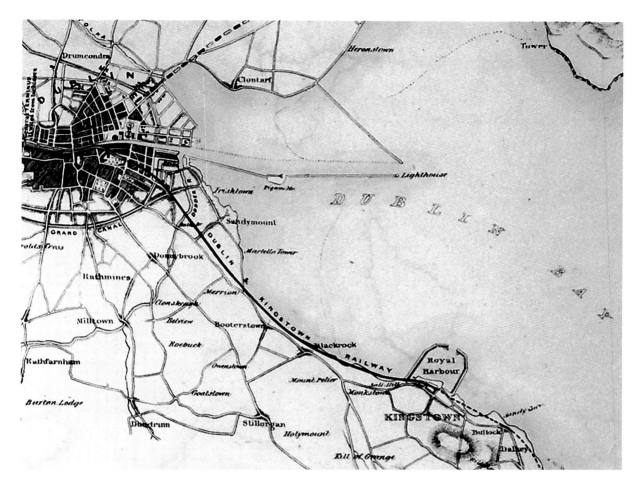

as 'T rails with button top and square flat bottom; the exterior or surface of the
rails to be made of the best hammered iron and the interior of the best puddle
iron'. A transverse granite sleeper was placed at intervals to maintain the gauge.
However, Vignoles experimented with a different arrangement during construction. A 200 m section of track along by the Grand Canal Dock area was laid
with longitudinal timber sleepers. The design of track in those days was truly at
an experimental stage and problems emerged with the selected system of granite
blocks on shingle. When the railway began operation this rigid foundation was
seen to play havoc with the suspension of the trains, damaging axles and springs.
In turn the pounding resulted in differential settlement which led to twist of the
track. The attrition also loosened the chairs and their fastenings. The *Penny
Cyclopedia* of 1838 informed that 'the lack of elasticity in these supports causes
the engines to work harshly'. Vignoles, always uneasy about the then orthodoxy
of the rigid track, was now fully converted to the virtues of elasticity. The initial
limited timber sleeper system had been shown to perform well. The granite
blocks were substituted by longitudinal timber sleepers that were placed under
the rail, thus providing a continuous support. A bridge rail (an inverted 'u' section) was introduced, secured onto the timber by spikes. This was the same tech-

Left. At Blackrock, still to be seen in the walkway: an original granite 'throughgoing block' of the D & KR of 1834 vintage. These cross-sleepers were used to maintain the 4 ft 8½ in gauge and were inserted at 'every fifth yard.'

At the Transport Museum in Cultra:
Below left. One of the original D & KR granite blocks, complete with cast iron chair.
Below. Cross-section and side elevation of rail attributed as being the original type used on the D & KR.
(Ulster Folk & Transport Museum)

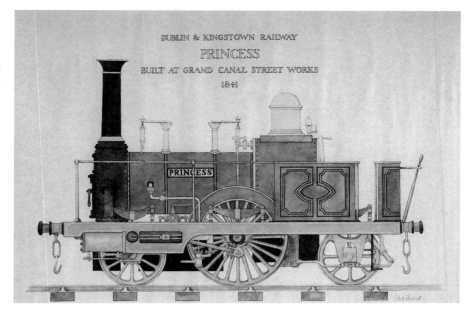

DUBLIN & KINGSTOWN RAILWAY
PRINCESS
BUILT AT GRAND CANAL STREET WORKS
1841

nique that Brunel had employed on his Great Western Railway in England. The granite blocks were progressively replaced and by December 1839 the track system had been completely changed.

And so, with the first line in place, the permanent way came to Ireland. Nothing in life is ever permanent, much less so the 'permanent way'. Regarding maintenance and renewal, there is always a need for a squad of people to keep the railway right. One can envisage these men, spread out along the coast, maintaining this new fangled railway, despite the occasional blast of cold seawater blown by the mercurial east winds from the Irish Sea. From the very start of operation of the railway, constant attention was needed. The men had to dig back the sand and pack up the granite blocks, as well as refix the loose fastenings of the chairs. The mission for the permanent way men was the same then as it is today: that of keeping the line open, as well as providing a safe and smooth ride for the railway passengers. As we have seen, after the opening of the line, the replacement of the granite blocks had to be carried out. It is likely that this heavy work was carried out in the period after the trains stopped in the evening and before the first train in the morning. Beech and memel (from Memel, now Klaipeda, on the Baltic) and latterly a yellow pine were used for the timber sleepers. The granite blocks were reused in strengthening the sea embankments and parapets along the line and in paving the promenades.

As part of his contract, Dargan had to maintain the track for two years. Then the D & KR had to set up its own maintenance section. Amongst the 237 employees of the D & KR listed in 1856, in addition to a number of labourers, were two engineers and 12 platelayers. The track was split up into three 'Divisions': the 'Dublin', with 1 ½ miles of double track; the 'Central' and the 'Kingstown', with 2 ½ miles each. Each of these was staffed by a foreman and three platelayers. K. A. Murray, in his informative book, tells us that there was a

Left. A grand hurrah at the opening of the D & KR, as the train leaves the Westland Row terminus. (Ulster Folk & Transport Museum)

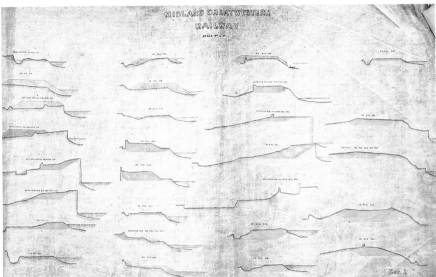

Left. Engineering sections on a drawing used during the construction of the Midland Great Western Railway from Dublin to Enfield. (Iarnród Éireann)

Left. The Dargan Saloon. William Dargan was a prodigious builder of the railways in Ireland, beginning with the construction of the D & KR. He used this special railway carriage (constructed in 1844) for his work. (Ulster Folk & Transport Museum)

Above. A revolutionary change in the mode of transport: from the horse to the locomotive. The Dublin & Drogheda Railway at Baldoyle in 1844. (Ulster Folk & Transport Museum)

Right. The opening of the Great Southern & Western Railway in 1849, Mallow station.

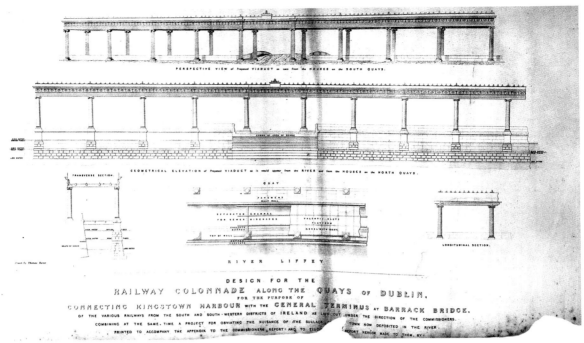

PERSPECTIVE VIEW of Proposed Viaduct as seen from the HOUSES on the SOUTH QUAYS.

GEOMETRICAL ELEVATION of Proposed Viaduct as it would appear from the RIVER and from the HOUSES on the NORTH QUAYS.

TRANSVERSE SECTION.

QUAY

LONGITUDINAL SECTION.

R I V E R   L I F F E Y

DESIGN FOR THE
RAILWAY COLONNADE ALONG THE QUAYS OF DUBLIN,
FOR THE PURPOSE OF
CONNECTING KINGSTOWN HARBOUR WITH THE GENERAL TERMINUS AT BARRACK BRIDGE,
OF THE VARIOUS RAILWAYS FROM THE SOUTH AND SOUTH-WESTERN DISTRICTS OF IRELAND AS LAID OUT UNDER THE DIRECTION OF THE COMMISSIONERS,
COMBINING AT THE SAME TIME A PROJECT FOR OBVIATING THE NUISANCE OF THE BULLAGE OF THE TOWN NOW DEPOSITED IN THE RIVER.
PRINTED TO ACCOMPANY THE APPENDIX TO THE COMMISSIONERS' REPORT AND TO ELUCIDATE REPORT HEREON MADE TO THEM, BY

Above. The yet-to-be-fulfilled dream of a route connecting the terminus at Westland Row directly to a general terminus for the west (now at Kingsbridge). This had early roots: a drawing dating from 1837 shows a colonnade carrying a proposed railway along the Liffey quays. (Iarnród Éireann)

Left. A photograph, from 1863, of a 'mock-up' bridge erected across Westmoreland Street, as seen from Trinity College. This demonstration of a proposed connecting Dublin Metropolitan Railway was not a success. It is reported that part of the scaffolding fell on a passer-by. (IRRS)

BOYNE VIADUCT.

Above. Original Contract drawing, Boyne Viaduct. Construction proved difficult due to complications in securing good foundations. It opened in 1855. (Iarnród Éireann)

Right. Diagram showing the renewal history of the track on the line around Drogheda, including the Boyne Viaduct. It shows the original inverted 'u' bridge rails used on the railway. Flat-bottom rails were installed from the late 1870s. (Ulster Folk & Transport Museum)

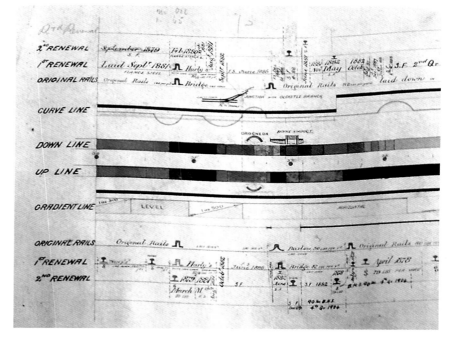

Below. An early example of the flat-bottom rail developed by Charles Blacker Vignoles. In Europe the modern version of the flat-bottom rail is known as the 'Vignoles' rail. (Irish Railway Record Society, IRRS)

THE EARLY FORM OF THE 'VIGNOLES RAIL.'

prize of £10 on offer in 1842 for the best maintained division. This was a prize worth securing, considering that the foreman's weekly wage was 12 shillings and that of a platelayer was ten shillings. This prize concept was one that continued into the mid-twentieth century. Another concept that has continued is that of walking and inspecting the line. However, one of its manifestations has not been continued. When it was planned to make a special inspection, the Board of the railway would convene at 6 am for breakfast at the Salthill Hotel. Then these pillars of the community would walk the line into Dublin.

So the railway age dawned. The D & KR proved to be a successful and profitable enterprise. The railway patently was the great new invention of its time, offering economic development and rich returns. Promoters rushed to present schemes for this wonderful manifestation of the age, and this development continued, despite the pall cast by the Famine in the 1840s. Belfast and Ulster emerged as the industrial powerhouse of the developing Victorian age in Ireland, and began to outstrip the rest of the country. It was thus appropriate that the next railway constructed was a section from Belfast to Lisburn, which was completed in August 1839. The Dublin & Drogheda Railway, in turn, was part of an overall intent to have a link between the two main cities in Ireland. John MacNeill, who was to be one of the pioneers of the art and science of engineer-

Left. The Bray Head section, designed by Isambard Kingdom Brunel, proved to be difficult terrain for the construction of a railway. Photograph taken after a derailment on 23rd April 1865, showing damage to the left of the timber trestle viaduct. The rails are bridge rails laid on longitudinal timber sleepers. The track gauge is maintained by transverse timber pieces placed at intervals. (Derek Paine)

Above right. The line at Bray Head has had to be moved inland on three occasions, due to erosion from the sea. At the beginning of the 20th century a new tunnel was constructed. Excavating the southern approach to No. 4 Tunnel on Bray Head in 1914. (Derek Paine)

Left. Photograph taken during the construction of No. 4 Tunnel. The 991 metre-long tunnel was completed in 1917. W. H. Hinde, resident engineer, is on the left. (Derek Paine)

Right. The south entrance to the tunnel in 1914 with Inspector W. Mc Garry pictured. (Derek Paine)

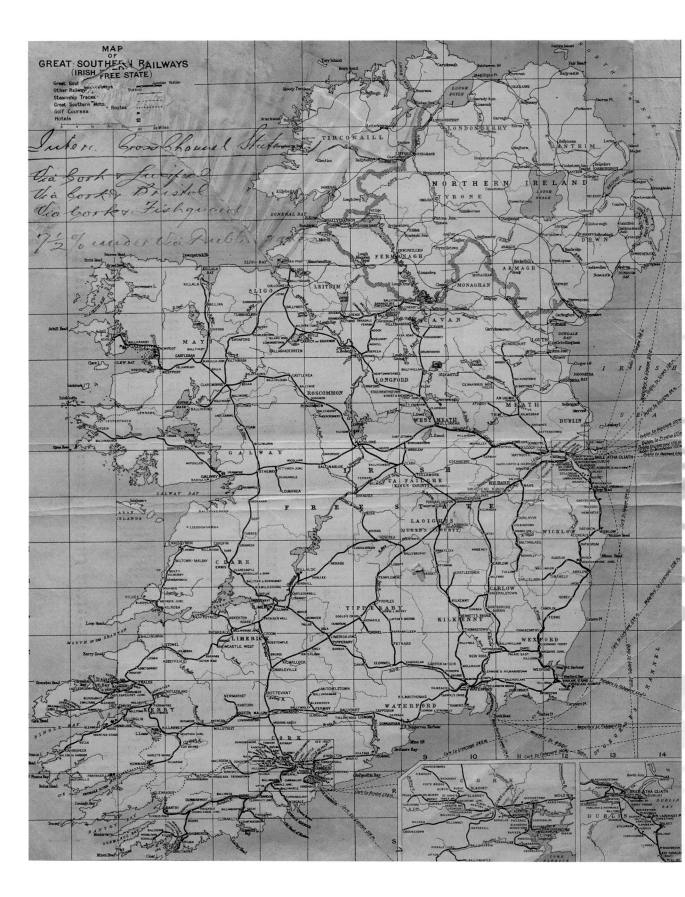

MAP
OF
GREAT SOUTHERN RAILWAYS
(IRISH FREE STATE)

Great Southern Railways
Other Railways
Steamship Tracks
Great Southern "Motor" Routes
Golf Courses
Hotels

Junction Station
Station

Inter. Cross Channel Rout

Via Cork & Liverpool
Via Cork & Bristol
Via Cork & Fishguard

7½% under via Dublin

Left. Map of the Irish railways in the late 1920s. By 1910 the railway system had reached its apogee, with a total length of 6,700 km in 1,600 mm gauge plus 800 km of narrow gauge. (Iarnród Éireann)

Right. The Civil War had a severe effect on the Irish railways. There was widespread destruction of bridges and track. In 1923, the five-arch masonry Ballyvoyle Viaduct, on the Waterford-Mallow line, was blown up. (Iarnród Éireann)

Right. A temporary track used to recover derailed rolling stock at Ballyvoyle. The viaduct was rebuilt later in 1923 using steel lattice girders. (Iarnród Éireann)

Above. As the damage inflicted on the railway intensified, a Railway Protection, Repair and Maintenance Corps was formed at the end of 1922. Armoured locomotive 'Tutankhamen' of the Corps at Mullingar. (IRRS)

Left. Trains were derailed several times at Killurin, in the Enniscorthy-Wexford section, during the Civil War. A rail that was removed is seen to the left. (Liam Brennan)

Right. Men of the Corps can be seen among those engaged in repairs at the damaged Belvelly Viaduct (south of Fota) on the Cork-Queenstown (now Cobh) line. (IRRS)

Right. Damaged Underbridge 41 on the Mallow-Tralee line, propped by a sleeper crib in July 1923. (Plumer Collection)

Near right. The damaged fourth arch of Carrig Viaduct on the Waterford-Mallow line, in July 1923. Repairs underway with centering erected.

Far right. December 1922, taking out girders of Underbridge 87 on the Dublin-Cork line. (Plumer Collection)

Left. A steam crane, at work rerailing a derailed wagon, under the protection of the Army. (IRRS)

THE COUNTY DONEGAL RAILWAYS
JOINT COMMITTEE.

PUBLIC NOTICE.

On **SATURDAY, 26th FEBRUARY, 1921,**
a number of large boulders were placed on the Railway near Ballinamore
Station on the

STRANORLAR & GLENTIES LINE

to obstruct the passage of Trains, and on the same day, and at a point between
Fintown and Glenties, a rail was removed, the track was torn up, and so
diverted as to result in a Train being thrown off the Line and precipitated
down the embankment into the lake alongside. From information received it
is clear this was the work of miscreants living in the immediate vicinity.

The action of the cowardly criminals who perpetrated the above might
have caused a calamitous accident, and involved the death of the Railwaymen
concerned with the working of the Train, as well as the Passengers, and this is
to give Notice that if there is any further interference with the Railway the

STRANORLAR AND GLENTIES LINE
WILL BE

CLOSED

For **ALL TRAFFIC** without further Notice.

Any information that will lead to the identification of the guilty parties will
be thankfully received by the undersigned.

HENRY FORBES, Traffic Manager.

STRANORLAR.

Left. Disturbances also occurred during the War of Independence: in this example, in February 1921, boulders were placed on the line between Fintown and Glenties, where a malicious derailment also took place. Here, in this poster, Henry Forbes, traffic manager of the County Donegal Railways, threatens the closure of operations on the Stranolar and Glenties line if there is any further interference with the railway. (Ulster Folk & Transport Museum)

ing in Ireland, had been appointed as the company's engineer. Work on a southern section began in 1838, and after some fitful starts the partial completion of the line to Drogheda from Dublin was marked by a special train, which ran in May 1844. The track was composed of timber sleepers laid transversely (the arrangement of sleepers in general use today) on which were fixed bridge rails.

Lack of joined-up-thinking can be a serious matter when it comes to track gauge. The initial line of the Ulster Railway, out of Belfast, had been laid at a gauge of 6 ft 2 in (2,340 mm), as recommended by the second report of the Railway Commissioners in 1838. The Dublin & Drogheda had originally intended to use the 6 ft 2 in gauge but MacNeill, after consulting with engineers in England, had a change of mind by 1842. The directors of the Dublin & Drogheda Railway accepted MacNeill's recommendation of a gauge of 5 ft 2 in (1,575 mm) in January 1843. This now raised the spectre that there could be three railway gauges in the country, including the 4 ft 8½ in of the D & KR. The need to have a through service from Dublin to Belfast made it self-evident that a unified gauge was needed. The Inspector General of Railways, Major General Pasley, was asked by the Board of Trade to come up with a solution. He consulted widely with experts, including George Stephenson. In Britain at the time there were several gauges under consideration: in addition to the 4 ft 8½ in these included 5 ft and 5 ft 6 in. A seminal moment occurred when Pasley discussed the issue with railway engineers and locomotive manufacturers in Britain and asked them if a mean of 5 ft 3 in (1,600 mm) would work. They assured him it would and arising from this deliberate and evaluative approach, he chose this gauge for Ireland in March 1843. It was confirmed by the Gauge of Railways Act in August 1846.

Thus was born the unique 'Irish' gauge, which is still in use across the island. Incidentally, it was also introduced to railways in South Australia and Brazil, and is still in use there. Ironically, each of these networks is much greater than the Irish one. In Australia it was introduced by an Irish railway engineer, Francis Webb Shields, in 1854. In 1863 the first railway constructed in New Zealand followed, what was at that time for them, the Australian orthodoxy of 5 ft 3 in. However, it was changed to a new national gauge of 3 ft 6 in (1,067 mm) around 1877. The locomotives and rolling stock were sold to the railways in Australia, but much of these were lost when the ship carrying these was wrecked. In Brazil, the 5 ft 3 in gauge was used on a series of railways, the first of which was inaugurated in 1867. There is a report that Thomas Grendon & Company of Drogheda manufactured and supplied an Irish gauge steam locomotive to Brazil in 1885.

The 6 ft 2 in portion of the Ulster Railway was changed to the new 5 ft 3 in gauge in 1849 and the D & KR was converted to the new gauge in 1855. The last link on the Dublin to Belfast route was the difficult crossing of the deep and wide valley formed by the Boyne River at Drogheda. The magnificent Boyne Viaduct, which bridged the gap despite severe difficulties in construction, was finally given approval to carry traffic in April 1855.

By now, railways serving the main radial routes out of Dublin were being built at a frenetic pace. The Great Southern & Western Railway's main Dublin to Cork line was completed by December 1855. Tralee was reached by 1859. The Midland Great Western Railway built a magnificent terminus at Broadstone in Dublin, in the Egyptian style. Mullingar was reached in 1848 and the line to Galway was opened in 1851. To the southeast, Waterford had a railway connection by 1854.

By the commencement of the 1870s there were just over 3,200 km of 1,600 mm track in the country. In the two decades that followed, a series of narrow gauge lines were built. Cheaper to construct, the development of those along the western seaboard in disadvantaged areas was encouraged by a subsidy funded by local rates. By 1910, the number of railway lines had reached its apogee. There was a total track of around 6,700 km (including sidings) in 1,600 mm gauge plus nearly 800 route km in narrow gauge (including some that were steam or electric tramways).

The railways were well built, a legacy we still enjoy today. There were great cuttings, embankments, tunnels and viaducts, carrying the trains at reasonable gradients through the undulating Irish countryside. Ireland is shaped like a bowl, flat in the middle with, generally, mountains on the periphery. The railway builders conquered all. Bray Head (in the Bray to Greystones section) is the epitome of the engineer's art in taming wild nature. The railway passes under high cliffs, over ramparts towering above the ever restless sea, over bridges and through a series of tunnels. Here the battle with nature is ongoing. The track has been moved inland three times since the railway was driven through, initially to the design of Isambard Kingdom Brunel.

The flat lands in the centre of Ireland also offered challenges. The railway had to be laid over bogland. Some 10% of the total railway in Ireland runs over bog. A bog is not inert; it is a living organic mass, very dependent on its water content, and in its natural state, amounts to around 95% of water. The construc-

Above. The Bretland Tracklayer lifting the down road near Lake Owel on the Sligo line, around 1925. Innovative for its time, it was developed by the Chief Engineer of the MGWR, Arthur Bretland. (Neilus O' Donoghue)

Left. A Platov Tracklayer on Estonian Railways. This machine, developed by the railways of the Soviet Union, operates on the same principles as the Bretland Tracklayer, developed 70 years beforehand. (Pat Jennings)

Right. Native timber was used for sleepers during the First World War, seen here being hauled for the GNR (I). This timber tended to rot and over the years, where possible, timber for sleepers was imported. (IRRS)

Right. Permanent way men pose on the track at Baltinglass Station. (IRRS)

Right. In County Antrim in the early part of the 20th century it is time for a break during the work: the kettle is about to be placed on the fire, as the engineer looks on. The crew of the Northern Counties Committee locomotive also observe. (Ulster Folk & Transport Museum)

tion commenced by carrying out extensive drainage works. An embankment was built using heather sods laid on dried peat. Clay and gravel fill were laid on this. Settlements were a continuing occurrence but this was made up with more lightweight fill.

The track system eventually evolved into the arrangement we know today. The Dublin & Drogheda Railway, when built, had employed bridge rails, but with transverse timber sleepers. In 1876 the line came under the Great Northern Railway (Ireland) which converted the rails to flat-bottom steel rails, again on transverse wooden sleepers. Charles Blacker Vignoles is credited with the general introduction of the flat-bottomed rail in 1836. It is still known on the European continent as 'Vignoles' rail. While the rest of the Irish railways generally used bullhead rail (rail with a head and foot of similar shape), the Midland Great Western Railway (MGWR) used flat-bottom rail from the start. One of our interviewees relates how the rails used in the MGWR were heavier than the equivalents used in the German railways, where both the frequencies and speeds of trains were much higher.

The earliest type of rail used in mine railways was made of cast iron. Cast iron is poor in tension and this limited the lengths that could be used. Wrought iron is made from pig iron mixed with slag. Some of the slag remains when it is

Above. The original wrought iron trusses of the Boyne Viaduct at Drogheda were replaced by a steel structure in 1932. (IRRS)

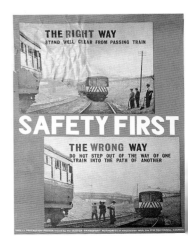

Above. March 1924: assorted dignitaries pose at the opening of the bascule lifting railway bridge over the Bann at Coleraine on the Belfast-Derry line.
Right. Square crossing at Dundalk, in place until 1953. The line from the 'Irish North' crossed two mainline tracks and continued to Barrack Street and on to Greenore.
Left. Safety poster for permanent way staff produced by the Ulster Transport Authority. (Ulster Folk & Transport Museum)

Above. Cross-girders from Underbridge 44 on the Loop line, being reconditioned at Inchicore Railway works in Dublin. This bridge over the Liffey underwent a programme of renewal between 1958 and 1960. (Iarnród Éireann)

Left. Installation of a footbridge at Dún Laoghaire in 1957. (Iarnród Éireann)

Above. June 1960: a gang of permanent way men pack the track in advance of the first tamper, the Matisa, on the Dublin to Cork line. Inspector Gerry O' Mahony, in the hat, supervises. (National Library of Ireland)

Right. Plasser Duomatic tamper in 1969. It could tamp two sleepers at a time. The use of on-track machines marked a great advance in productivity. (National Library of Ireland)

Left. By the middle of the 20th century there were widespread closures of railway lines. Ready for lifting: the track at Carrickmines on the closed Harcourt Street line in 1960. Permanent way men travel down the overgrown track using a rail-mounted tractor. This system was effective but slow. It could take a week to lift a mile. (National Library of Ireland)

rolled and this gives it a fibrous structure. The fibrous structure meant that when used in rail, it performed better in tension and thus longer lengths could be made. Wrought or 'rolled' iron formed the composition of the rails used on the early Irish railways. There is a report that the first steel rails were rolled at the Ebbw Vale works in Wales in 1855. Following the development of the Bessemer smelting process in 1857, steel became available in larger quantities and correspondingly less expensive. Steel rails performed better and were gradually introduced, reflecting the drop in their price. As locomotives grew in size and with faster train speeds, rails became heavier.

The railways in Ireland ranged all over the country, eventually reaching many remote localities. A railway is a huge, complex enterprise and is a labour intensive undertaking. It brought steady and valuable employment to parts of the country where hitherto there was only intermittent income from agriculture. The railways were the technologically advanced industry of their time. They spread technical and organisational expertise all over Ireland. And thus, throughout the country, teams of men were dedicated to maintaining the tracks so as to allow these trains to travel at unprecedented speed and with regularity. There were permanent way men in every county in Ireland. Many came from farms, and had to adapt to the new discipline of a fixed day and adhering to schedules, such as working between train paths. The hard physical work involved would not have been a problem; they would have been used to that. And so, the hierarchical permanent way organisation came into place: platelayers, gangers, permanent way inspectors, and, at the top of the hierarchy, the engineer.

Below. Jeremiah Coleman working on the removal of the track of the West Cork railway during the early 1960s. (Bernard Coleman)

Right. The demise of the West Cork railway: seen in 1964, a rail lifting train on the Chetwynd Viaduct in the Cork to Bandon section. (National Library of Ireland)

Below. An auction of items, including rails, from the closed Donegal railways, in March 1961. (Ulster Folk & Transport Museum)

The Permanent Way Institution was founded in 1884. It covered Britain, Ireland, and the then colonies. Amongst the first members listed are an A. Hamilton-Smythe, district engineer, of the MGWR in Athlone and a M. Fannon, permanent way inspector, also of Athlone. The Permanent Way Institution has played a valuable role in the history and discipline of permanent way. By its nature it is a specialised subject and the meetings held by the Institution offer a forum for papers given in various aspects of the discipline. Representatives of all grades attend the meetings. There is a very active social side to the institution; it affords members from all over the country the opportunity to mix and share perhaps, a cup of tea or occasionally, another beverage. There are regular overseas trips with visits to various advanced technical track installations in railways.

Maintaining or renewing the permanent way is a tough business. It involves hard physical work. All the main components are heavy: the rail, sleepers and fastenings. In comparison with a construction site, the railway one is different: elongated for hundreds of kilometres, a workspace that can measure just metres across, with heavy trains travelling past at up to 160 kph. For more than the first hundred years on the Irish railway, all of the activity was physical. It entailed large squads of men, digging, packing and shovelling. There was lifting and plac-

Above. The Chief Engineer's Department, 1957. Front, from left: D. Herlihy, P. T. Somerville Large, J. Hyde Ffolliott. Back, T. S. Harman, A. M. Plumer, J. Meleady. (Iarnród Éireann)

ing sleepers. To lift a length of rail up into a wagon properly required a well-drilled choreography, as some of our interviewees tell later. Directed by the inspector, everyone of the 30 men involved in lifting a rail length moved precisely to the four stages of command, starting with 'Hands on' and ending with 'Fire'.

It was a healthy life, despite being out in all weathers. By definition, to survive in this environment you had to be fit. Work was set out, with quotas like shovelling out ballast from a certain number of wagons per day. Beater packing meant packing the ballast under sleepers, again with set lengths to be achieved.

Work was carried out between the passage of trains, with flagmen sent out each side of the works. It is difficult to imagine now, how this was arranged and communicated, in an era before the mobile phone. In those days, intricate work was planned and the signalman informed. Various stratagems were devised, for example, an extra tail lamp put on a train was meant to warn the permanent way men that there was an additional special train. Permanent way inspectors threw their messages to gangs from the footplates of passing trains. It was difficult to get around. There were no vans or cars. The railway is usually located in remote terrain, away from main roads. Materials were delivered to the work site by train. The men came to work by their own devices, such as by bicycle, using handy

Above. Relaying gang at the 58 milepost, Dublin-Cork line, in 1941. Thomas Donovan is second from right. (Dan Donovan)

Left. The Matisa tamper, with sleeping car in tow, in transit through Cork from Albert Quay to Glanmire station. (Colm Creedon)

Far left. Using a T wrench to tighten fang bolts in the 'gullet', on the gradient from Heuston Station towards Inchicore. (Iarnród Éireann)

Near left. Taking off rails in Cork Tunnel. From left: Gerry Healy, John O' Brien, Mick Mulcahy. (Vernon Kiely)

bicycle paths along the side of the track that they had devised. Inspectors and chief inspectors might inspect the line or travel to a work site on the single or double rail bicycle.

Conditions were tough in the early days; there was no issuance of weatherproof jackets or hats. Work wear like safety boots or gloves were not issued. Health and safety has improved significantly over the last couple of decades. However, there always was a healthy and strict respect for the safety of trains. Indeed keeping the trains running safely has been the leitmotif of the permanent way man.

There was a rigid hierarchy in a spartan organisation. The engineer was seen to be thrifty, remote, lofty and tough, given to issuing delphic decrees. Waste and bad work were not tolerated. Many of the early engineers came from an Anglo-Irish background. They were excellent railway engineers. Relations between the top level and the workforce were very formal, a usual feature of an organisation founded in Victorian times. The chief permanent way inspector was almost a god-like creature, keeping a sharp eye on all the men to ensure that they were carrying out their duties and maintaining the quality of the track. The permanent way inspector and the ganger were hard taskmasters who did not tolerate slacking and extracted the last from the men. Everyone knew his place in this exacting environment, and accepted this as normal.

During the 19th century, engineers were polymaths who 'engineered' many things. Brunel was the outstanding example. He designed and built bridges, railways and steamships. Engineering has always been important and the Chief Civil Engineer's Department is at the heart of the railway. It is one of the essential elements without which the railway cannot function. In the world of Irish engineering, the railways have been pioneers in introducing advanced techniques. They have always been on the lookout to do it quicker, smarter, and

The construction of the DART was a major project which began in 1980.

Above. Renewing track at Dalkey.
Above left. 1981, from left: David Waters, who directed the DART project, discusses progress with Permanent Way Inspector Dan Donovan and CIÉ General Manager Jack Higgins.
Left. Relaying near Grand Canal Docks in October 1980.

(Iarnród Éireann)

Above. Renewal of Rogerstown Viaduct on the Dublin to Belfast line in 1986. Two steam cranes lift in the pre-stressed concrete beams.

cheaper. Over the years, the railways have been to the forefront in employing new construction technology in Ireland such as mass, then reinforced and pre-stressed concrete. It is noteworthy that Engineers Ireland, itself celebrating its 175th anniversary in 2010, counted prominent railway engineers among its founders, which presaged the close association that engineers from the railway had with that institution in the years that followed.

During the Civil War of 1922-23 the Irish railways became embroiled in the conflict. Being an essential part of the economy and society, a railway is a very visible symbol. And so track and bridges were blown up and trains were derailed. In Bernard Share's book *In Time of Civil War* he relates the quote that 'The attitude towards the Civil War of the railwaymen was...politically neutral. But was marked by a loyalty to their profession...' Permanent way men did their best to adapt to the new reality, and kept on with the task of keeping the system capable of running trains. They repaired track and bridges, they helped to re-rail locomotives. Permanent Way Inspector Michael Forde of Wexford was prominent in getting the line open all his area where there were many derailments. There is a report that, in a raid at Churchill station in County Donegal, two gangs of permanent way men were kidnapped by 'Irregulars' in July 1922. In August 1922 a permanent way train with its equipment was captured. A Railway Protection, Repair, and Maintenance Corps was formed by the Free State Government during the last months of 1922. In addition to including men trained in weaponry, railway staff were recruited. This allowed temporary repairs to be made under military protection. An interesting vignette, which illustrates the low wages pertaining to permanent way staff at that time, was the suggestion in a note by a Government Minister, in the context of keeping expenditure to a minimum, that enrolment in the Corps be restricted to 'permanent way men and porters'. The mayhem inflicted on the railways during the Civil War was so great that the Corps eventually reached a strength of over 3,000 men.

The railway in Ireland was bedevilled by lack of investment at many times during the 20th century. By the beginning of that century, the construction of new lines had ground to a halt. The construction of 58 km of line between Rosslare Strand and Waterford, completed in 1906, represented the last major

expansion. By the end of the First World War, the internal combustion engine had reached new levels of sophistication. The growth in numbers of cars, buses and trucks, along with the development of improved roads to cater for them, added up to a great competitive threat to the railways. The Irish railways began to consolidate from the 1930s. The major cutbacks came in the late 1950s and onwards when around 1,600 route km were closed.

Against this background, the railways continued, managing to endure despite a lack of money. It is a tribute to all who worked in Irish railways that they have managed to survive and keep them going, despite this unpromising environment. In running a railway, the permanent way is a significant part of the expenditure. Thus it was that funds were always tight. New materials were hard to come by. There were several waves of frugality, mirroring the hard economic times Ireland had undergone since independence. There was little money available during the Economic War, in the period after the First World War. Then there was the Second World War, or the 'Emergency' as it was euphemistically called. Incidentally, the railways proved their worth during these times, carrying people and goods all over the country. In post-war Ireland, the economy was slow to take off. In turn, it was only in the 1970s that real new investment in the track began to be made, with major relaying carried out on the Cork line. The staff of the permanent way, always supremely adaptable, learned to keep the railway going. If new materials were available these were placed in the important mainlines. The old rails and sleepers that were recovered were cascaded to the

Above. Plasser & Theurer 08-16 tamper. This consolidates, lines and levels the track. (Iarnród Éireann)

Below. The tines of the tamper compact the ballast under the sleeper. (Iarnród Éireann)

Right. At Dublin docks in 1985: importation of 54 kg rails in long lengths. The rail wagons travel along by the end of the East Link Bridge to pass by the side of the Point Depot. (Iarnród Éireann)

secondary branch lines. In some cases this material (now third hand) was later on transferred and used in the lowest category lines. 'Mend and make do' was the order of the day. Another source of material arose due to the retrenchment of the Irish railways. The various waves of line closures meant that rails and sleepers were salvaged, if serviceable. Everything possible was reused, including bridges.

However, enlightened management recognised the obvious – without a decent track one did not have a railway. To quote the then General Manager of CIÉ, Jack Higgins, in a paper delivered in 1979, 'the efficient operation of any railway is completely dependent on the state of the track'. Following a cost-benefit analysis carried out in 1976, the Dublin-Cork line was renewed with continuous welded rail and concrete sleepers. This was a sea change and allowed higher speeds and reduced maintenance costs. The renewal exercise continued up to the end of the 1980s.

An upgrade of the Dublin suburban line was necessary. Much of the track was life-expired, as were the trains serving this suburban network. Investment in what was to be called the DART (Dublin Area Rapid Transit) system was approved in the late 1970s. This project for a modern electrified urban train service entailed a significant number of improvements, including renewal of most of the track. New bridges were built or raised to accommodate the electrified lines. Platforms and stations were upgraded. State-of-the-art signalling was installed and a depot was converted and extended to accommodate the modern DART fleet. When the DART opened in 1984, it could be seen that at last real investment had been made in the Irish railways. The public responded to the high quality service that the DART provided and it has been embraced as a fundamental aspect of Dublin life.

The next important focus was on the Belfast line. It coincided with the improvement in North-South relationships and the funding that emerged from this. Major renewal of the Dublin to Belfast line began in the mid 1990s. It was considered as a prioritised project. Bridges were raised where necessary. A special depot was set up in Drogheda and the work north to the border was complete

Left. Upgrading work on the Derry line was carried out in the period 2008-2009. On the left, installing a crossover. On the right, tightening bolts of a fishplate. (Northern Ireland Railways)

by 1997. The track north of the border was upgraded by Northern Ireland Railways (NIR). A new, rebranded, 'Enterprise' train, a joint venture between Iarnród Éireann and NIR was announced. Using new rolling stock from De Dietrich, improved services ran over the upgraded track.

The accident at Knockcroghery (north-west of Athlone) in 1997 was a seminal event. Here, a passenger train was derailed, the cause being degraded track. Thankfully, nobody was injured. As it happened, the event occurred near to Athlone, the home base of the then Minster for Transport Mary O'Rourke, who was to prove very supportive of the railway and the quest to radically improve safety. Iarnród Éireann commissioned the consultants A. D. Little to look at railway safety. In turn a consultant firm, IRMS, was commissioned in April 1998 by the Government to review railway safety. Both reports coincided in making recommendations on improving both the physical assets of Iarnród Éireann as well as the 'softer' elements such as safety management systems and training. Amongst other things, the IRMS report noted that the rail in some locations was over 100 years old and was inadequate. Iarnród Éireann responded by developing a series of five-year Railway Safety Programmes, which were accepted and funded by the Government. The first, the 1999-2003 Railway Safety Programme, made serious allocations for relaying the track. There was also some additional funding from the European Union. The permanent way men rose to the challenge. Previously, around 1990, the average length of track relaid was around 25 km per year. When the first Railway Safety Programme swung into action the relaying rate was brought to over 150 km per year, with all sections of the Infrastructure Department making herculean efforts. There was some satisfaction in replacing rails, in the west of Ireland, which were over 100 years old in some places, where there had never been relaying since the railway was built.

Right. Clockwise from below left: ultrasonic testing; tightening fastenings; upgrading the Sligo line, 1992; maintaining tampers at Kildare Depot; making concrete sleepers at Portlaoise Depot, (Iarnród Éireann) ; Thermit welding of rails at night on the Cork line, 2009. (Jim Shaw)

Left. A Luas light rail vehicle, adjacent to the former heavy rail terminus at Harcourt Street in Dublin. It is laid to standard gauge (1,435 mm). Here, the track is embedded in the street.

Investment continued with the second Railway Safety Programme which ended in 2008. By that stage a total of over 1,000 km of track had been re-laid on the radial routes (excluding the mainlines which had been relaid earlier) along with a host of other safety initiatives. Dr. John Lynch, Chairman of CIÉ since 2000, has presided over an unprecedented period of general investment, not seen since the construction of the railways in the mid-19th century. At last, the Irish railway has received real and sustained investment. In addition to the installation of modern continuously welded rail across the network already mentioned, there have been new stations, facilities and rolling stock. Old lines such as the Midleton line and the Ennis-Athenry line were completely reconstructed. An additional line has been laid to Hazelhatch as part of the Kildare Route Project. Increased frequencies and more comfortable trains led to Iarnród Éireann enjoying the greatest rise in passenger numbers among European railways. As the economic climate worsens, the period of increased railway investment made around the beginning of the 21st century, including improved track, will hopefully be a sound basis for Irish railways to continue through yet another economic downturn.

Below. The modern and the old. Bord na Móna operates a railway network of around 1,300 km, of which 850 km is permanent track. About five million tonnes of peat are transported annually. The gauge is 914 mm. Steel sleepers can be seen in the photograph on the left. (Bord na Móna)

Right. The Iarnród Éire-ann Track Recording Vehicle. This travels the network, using advanced technology to diagnose track condition. (Andy Byrne)

Northern Ireland Railways (NIR), a subsidiary of Translink, are an integral part of the Irish railway picture. NIR took over from the Ulster Transport Authority in 1968. There was a radical consolidation of the network in Northern Ireland, with a decline from 1,500 km in the mid-20th century to currently just over 320 km at present. The NIR network now essentially consists of the mainline from the border to Belfast as well as the lines to Bangor and Larne, with the long single line which reaches the north Antrim coast and loops around to Derry. Track was composed of jointed rail until the late 1970s, when a concerted programme was commenced to relay with CWR. The effects of the troubles affected the permanent way staff of NIR. Blown up track and bridges, as with the experiences during the Civil War in the south in the 1920s, it was part of the permanent way mission to go out speedily, get the track back into shape and reopen to traffic. Coming from the same genesis, there has always been a healthy spirit of cooperation between the two railways. The gauge is the same. The same trains run between the two jurisdictions operating to one rule book. Over the years specialised track maintenance machinery has been shared.

Other instances of steel wheel on rail transport in Ireland deserve mention in the story of the permanent way. There are several heritage railways, such as those in Tralee and Waterford, where volunteers maintain track and operate trains. Bord na Móna, in order to transport its milled peat, operates a network of around 1,300 km, 850 km of which is permanent. Steel sleepers are used and the gauge is 3 ft (914 mm). There is a record that the owner of an early Irish peat briquette works utilised a narrow-gauge locomotive for transport of peat around 1870.

The Luas light rail system, which commenced services in Dublin in June 2004, has proved to be a great success. Light rail vehicles operate on the standard gauge (1,435 mm) track which consists of a mix of embedded in-street rails, slabtrack and conventional CWR on ballast.

Below. Screen display of the Track Recording Vehicle. (Andy Byrne)

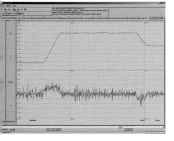

Government has always played a part in regulating safety on the railways. Under an 1842 Railways Regulation Act, no part of a railway could be opened unless inspected by a Railway Inspecting Officer. Under the Railway Safety Act 2005, a rigorous process for approval of new railway lines is in place. This is implemented by the Railway Safety Commission, which was established on the 1st January 2006.

Within the world of the permanent way there were two significant technical advances which marked a major leap forward. One was the introduction of CWR or continuous welded rail; the other was the introduction of mechanised track maintenance. Prior to the introduction of CWR, much of the maintenance work on the track was necessary at the joints between the rails. The fastenings, the fishplates, the bolts, the sleepers all got battered at the joint by the passage of the wheels of the train. Installing a continuous length of rail eliminated the need for joints. The concept had been developed in continental Europe with the installation there of CWR after the Second World War. The tendency of a long length of rail to buckle in heat or contract in cold temperatures was counteracted by strong fastenings and with the sleepers being embedded in restraining ballast. To minimise extremes due to variation in temperatures, the rail was stressed allowing it to be set at a mid-range temperature. The long length rails were joined in-situ using an aluminothermic welding process. From the early 1960s CIÉ engineers were sent abroad to railways to inspect CWR practice. This was also against the background of the need to introduce concrete sleepers which was a response to the poor quality of sleepers made from native Irish timber. In the mid 1960s a trial section of CWR was installed on the Cork Line near the 11 milepost. This was popularly called the 'Golden Mile'. The concept proved satisfactory and CWR began to be installed, initially on mainlines. Now, as we have seen, practically all the branch lines (as well as the mainlines) have this modern form of track. The clickety-clack is gone. Maybe it was a romantic concept for those prone to nostalgia. However the elimination of joints contributes to ride-comfort for the passengers, as well as doing away with the problem of battered rail joints that required major care and attention from the permanent way men.

For the first century of the railway practically all the permanent way tasks entailed hard physical work. There were some exceptions like the mechanical tracklayer employed by the Midland Great Western Railway developed by the

Spanning 175 years: the oldest and the most modern.
Above right. One of the first passenger coaches. A third-class carriage of the D & KR, from 1834. (Ulster Folk & Transport Museum)

Below right. A Class 22000 Rotem Inter-City Railcar of the 21st century. The permanent way, throughout the years, was built to carry all such traffic. (Iarnród Éireann)

Chief Engineer Arthur Bretland in 1923. Pre-assembled track panels could be brought to the relaying site. The old panels were taken out using the gantry of the tracklayer and the new panels lifted in. It is reported to have been capable of handling 800 metres of track in an eight-hour period. It was in use up to the Second World War. A copy of this was made in Britain and used on the LNER up to the 1960's and, possibly, inspired a similar tracklayer, the 'Platov' in use by the railways of the Soviet Union.

From around the mid-20th century, machinery of one kind or another began to be introduced on the Irish railways, which, little by little, made the tasks easier and began to reduce the heavy physical element. Rail saws and drills, attached to a basic motor, were introduced in the 1960s. The introduction of the humble Priestman crane to Irish railway maintenance was a great advance in lifting heavy weights such as rails and sleepers. The Matisa tamping machine was introduced in the 1950s. While men had to pack up the track in advance, the machine then packed the ballast under the sleeper. This eliminated the need to have beater packing (a technique of packing the ballast using an implement like a pick with a blunt edge.) The first of what we would consider a modern tamper came with the introduction of the Plasser and Theurer 04 tamper. It was faster and it did not require the track to be packed up in advance. Fast forward to today: a fleet of modern tampers is available for maintenance. Peak output of one of these is around 200 metres in an hour. These are highly sophisticated and can line and level the track, using an automatic lining system.

Other improvements included the Donelli gantry system. This was introduced in 1978 and brought relaying to an almost industrial output, enabling longer stretches of track to be relaid in a limited possession time. A Track Recording Vehicle diagnoses track quality and outputs data which can be downloaded to the computer of the engineer and permanent way inspector. Another diagnostic system is the ultrasonic testing of all rails in-situ. This identifies flaws in rails and helps to reduce the incidence of broken rails.

And yet, despite all these improvements in technology, there is a need for the permanent way staff. Maintaining the track is still a labour intensive activity. There remains the need to physically walk the track and inspect it. There is a need for people to speedily fix defects and attend to emergencies. For example, the effects of current climate change have meant that there are more extremes such as heavier rainfall in recent times, with the potential to affect the railway. Track has a finite life; there is always the requirement for renewal.

Of course, conditions have improved. Today's workers travel in vans, with separate compartments for equipment. Personal protective equipment is issued. Training has radically increased. There is an enhanced professionalism. However, when the emergency occurs, it is the permanent way man or woman, from platelayer to engineer, who are to be found out there, in driving rain, sleet or wind. They are doing what they do best, fixing the problem in the fastest possible time, to allow the trains with their passengers to get moving again. They show dedication, dependability and skill, which has been the hallmark of the permanent way during the first 175 years of the Irish railways.

Chapter 2
Storm Clouds over the New Century

By the beginning of the 20th century, the railways in Ireland had reached their peak. However, storm clouds were on the horizon. Competition from the road was to intensify, and there was to be an economic recession. A new threat also arose: the Civil War. Arthur Plumer tells the story of how the permanent way continued throughout those challenging times and beyond.

Arthur Plumer

'Forty Years on the Permanent Way in Southern Ireland'. This chapter is an extract from a paper read to the Irish Section of the Permanent Way Institution, 15th December 1961.

My father had worked in the Signalling and Telegraph Department of the Great Southern & Western Railway (GS & WR). In 1921, when I qualified as a civil engineer from Dublin University, I had been thinking of what sort of a job I would try and get, when to my surprise, the then Chief Engineer of the GS & WR, John Sides, offered me a job as a temporary engineering assistant at £3 per week, in the office of the district engineer at Limerick. I had always been interested in railways, partly through my father and I was very glad to accept the offer. I was told to report at 10.00 am on Monday 12th September.

I have never forgotten the first instructions from Mr. Prittie Perry, the district engineer. These were to travel the next day to Ardfert (which I had never heard of) but which is a very small station – the last before Tralee on the North Kerry branch. I was told to measure and examine the dimensions of the well at the station and then to take some levels in connection with the very primitive station drainage. Then, if I had time, I was to check the station yard survey and if I had any more time, I was to measure up the station buildings. On looking at the timetable, I found the only train left Limerick at 10.25 am, and I had only three or four hours for the work before getting the one and only train back,

Above left. Arthur Plumer in 1955. Then district engineer, based at Westland Row in Dublin, he retired from the railway in 1961. He died in 1970. (Plumer Collection)

which left me in Limerick at 9.00 pm. I didn't get any further than the well and a few drainage levels. Incidentally, I learnt the lesson of dressing suitably for the job to be done, because I went down the well on a ladder to examine it and ruined my clothes. A kindly station master's wife helped to clean me up and provided me with hot water and soap.

I subsequently learned that the district engineer had given orders for a wire to be sent to the permanent way inspector at Listowel which read 'Meet Plumer at Ardfert on arrival of 10.25 am ex Limerick tomorrow'. Unfortunately the girl at the Telegraph Office put a 'b' in my name and the inspector, never having heard of me, looked for the Limerick plumber on the train at Listowel and, not finding him, did not bother to go to Ardfert, and so I did not have his help or advice.

About June in the following year, I was informed that I had been appointed to a draughtsman vacancy in the office of the Cork district engineer, Mr. Montague Mandeville. These were, however, troubled times, and one day, having gone to some job on the Limerick-Waterford branch, I heard that trouble had broken out in Limerick and the trains were stopped. Fortunately an engine and van, making for Limerick, came along and my chainman and I travelled in the van with a number of railway employees also making for Limerick. I remember that we were held up at Killonan – the station before Limerick – by a tough looking man in a green uniform who brandished a hefty revolver. He examined each man in the van and when he came to me, he showed great interest in, and suspicion of, the field book which I was carrying. However, all was well and we duly arrived at the station to find the whole place closed up.

This state of affairs went on for a fortnight when myself and a newly found friend, who was a commercial traveller from Dublin, and who stayed for a few days every month in my digs, decided that we would try and make our way to Dublin. We had heard that trains were running to Dublin from Thurles. So one Monday, about noon, when the shooting was at its quietest, we started off on foot from Limerick for Limerick Junction. We arrived there in the evening, having got lifts here and there on baker's vans, cars etc, and stayed the night in the Railway Hotel at the station. We were the only two people staying in it that night, and you'll see in a moment why I mention this fact. The next day we started off for Thurles and decided to do the first part of the journey along the railway. We had only gone a few miles when we came on a gang of permanent way men who asked us who we were and where we were going. I told them who I was and then one of them told me we had better get off the railway and make for the road, as a gang of men were preparing to blow up a bridge a short distance further up the line. We did as we were told, and walked quite a few miles before three jarvey cars on their way from Tipperary to Thurles caught up on us. They were taking some Americans to Thurles to catch a train to Dublin. They had two empty seats which were offered to us at ten shillings each and we accepted. We learned from them that a large number of Americans had landed at Cobh on the Sunday, and were brought up by train on the Monday. Finding that they could get no further along the Dublin line than Limerick Junction, they

were brought in their train to Tipperary where they booked out the whole town, some sleeping in bathrooms, some on billiard tables, and other uncomfortable means of resting. Little did they know that there was a practically empty hotel only two miles away where, as I mentioned, my friend and I spent the night. We arrived in Thurles in the evening too late to get a train to Dublin, so completed our journey the following morning. On arrival I went and reported to the Chief Engineer, who seemed very pleased to get such news as I could give him of the state of affairs in Limerick. I should mention that all telegraph and telephone communications had been destroyed. He then brought me to Kingsbridge where I repeated my story to the General Manager, Mr. E. A. Neale.

I then took up duty in the Chief Engineer's drawing office, and did not go to Cork until the following January. During the six months or so that I remained in Dublin, I was concerned in several interesting jobs. I should tell you that fighting was going on all over the country at this time. As a sequel to my meeting with the gang north of Limerick Junction on the Tuesday I was sent down some time later with the district engineer, Mr. Booth, who was going to repair the bridge that had been blown up. My job was to measure up the damage to the bridge – a three-arch masonry structure over a small river – and return to the office to make a plan showing the damage.

During this period, I and the late Mr. Leonard, who was a pupil in the chief engineer's office, and an old college friend of mine, were sent to Mallow to make a complete survey at Mallow Viaduct. This had recently been blown up and, being a fairly high ten-arch masonry structure, the fallen stones formed quite an appreciable sized dam across the River Blackwater. A gap had been made in the centre to let the water through, but the level of the water up-stream was appreciably above the level down-stream. However, before I go further into this, I would like to tell you of one amusing incident on our journey from Kingsbridge to Mallow. The train was able to proceed only as far as Charleville, where, after some difficulty, Mr. Leonard and I managed to engage a car to take us to Mallow. We were well loaded up with a theodolite, level, staff, legs, plenty of

Right. Devastation: map produced by the GS & WR showing the damage wrought on it during the Civil War up to the end of 1922. (IRRS)

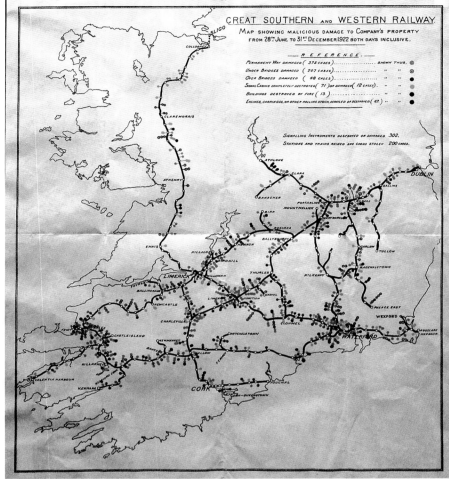

GREAT SOUTHERN AND WESTERN RAILWAY.

MAP SHOWING MALICIOUS DAMAGE TO COMPANY'S PROPERTY
FROM 28TH JUNE TO 31ST DECEMBER 1922 BOTH DAYS INCLUSIVE.

— REFERENCE —

PERMANENT WAY DAMAGED (375 CASES)	SHOWN THUS.	●
UNDER BRIDGES DAMAGED (207 CASES)	"	◉
OVER BRIDGES DAMAGED (48 CASES)	"	●
SIGNAL CABINS COMPLETELY DESTROYED (71) OR DAMAGED (12 CASES)	"	●
BUILDINGS DESTROYED BY FIRE (13)	"	●
ENGINES, CARRIAGES, OR OTHER ROLLING STOCK, DERAILED OR DESTROYED (47)	"	⬤

SIGNALLING INSTRUMENTS DESTROYED OR DAMAGED 302.
STATIONS AND TRAINS RAIDED AND GOODS STOLEN 200 CASES.

ranging poles and our personal luggage, as we expected to be some days on the job. When we got to the outskirts of Mallow, our car was stopped by a military patrol, and the first question we were asked was: 'Where are the Races?' Apparently, they mistook our red and white ranging poles for part of a bookmaker's equipment. The Chief Engineer had given us a special letter to the district engineer who lived outside Mallow to the south side of the river. We found our way to his house shortly before dark, and he very kindly invited us to stay and have a meal and a chat, with the result that it was quite dark when we started to try and find our way back to the hotel in the town. We could hear shooting going on all over the place, and I well remember feeling greatly relieved when we reached our destination. Our work was important as the plans we made were required for use in connection with the preparation of the design for the new viaduct. Incidentally, as a result of the destruction of the viaduct, a temporary station had to be provided at the south side of the river, and for some considerable time rail travellers and goods had to be conveyed by road between this station and the permanent station on the north side of the river.

There was one other interesting, and rather similar, job which was given to Mr. Leonard and myself by the Chief Engineer. A couple of miles on the Dungarvan side of Durrow station on the Waterford-Mallow line, the railway crosses a narrow glen on a viaduct on a place called Ballyvoyle. This had been a five-arch masonry structure, quite high in the middle and it had been completely destroyed. Again, we were sent down to make as accurate a survey as possible, which involved some interesting problems which we enjoyed solving. We were not within reasonable distance of any hotel, but we managed to persuade a local farmer to put us up. I remember how we enjoyed the good wholesome, well-cooked fare, especially after our hard days up and down the sides of the glen.

In 1923, I went to take up duty in Cork, and stayed there until April 1925. I look back upon that period with many happy memories, particularly because among those with whom I worked in the drawing office were the present civil engineer and the recently retired Cork district engineer. It was a busy time because a tremendous amount of reconstruction of destroyed and damaged bridges, station buildings, signal cabins etc. was in hand. I spent a considerable amount of my time in Kerry supervising various contractors who were engaged in these works.

In 1925, a very important event occurred in the history of the railways in the south. All were amalgamated or absorbed and the Great Southern Railways company was formed, which existed until 1944. So far as the Permanent Way Department was concerned, it was decided to have six districts with headquarters at Westland Row, Dublin: Broadstone, Dublin, Cork, Limerick, Waterford and Athlone. I was appointed assistant district engineer to Mr. J. Roberts at Athlone, and my other friends were appointed as follows – Mr. Somerville Large as assistant to Mr. Booth at Westland Row; Mr. Harman as assistant to Mr. Ffolliott at Broadstone and Mr. Leonard as assistant to Mr. Patterson at Waterford. It was very interesting going to a new district, particularly as most of it was ex MGWR, of which I knew nothing. They were indeed spacious days and one was able to devote plenty of time to the most important part of a per-

Above. The reconstructed Mallow Viaduct. The original masonry arch structure had been blown up during the Civil War in August 1922. At right, plaque comemorating the opening of the bridge by the President of the Executive Council, W. T. Cosgrave, October 1923. (Iarnród Éireann)

Below. The Bretland Tracklayer: it was used by Arthur Plumer on the Mallow-Waterford line. However this location turned out to be too far from the depot in Mullingar. (IRRS)

manent way engineer's work, i.e. inspection of the track. Apart from the absorbing interest of this type of work there is the healthy aspect. A day spent walking or riding on a rail cycle was a very enjoyable experience except under bad weather conditions.

During my Athlone days, I learnt a lot about and did a lot of realignment of curves. I also learnt to appreciate the beauty of the west, especially Connemara and west Mayo, and also the 'niceness' – I can't think of a more suitable word – of the people. Some of the bridge renewal jobs were unusually interesting and provided opportunity for learning the very important lessons that if you want to carry out a bridge renewal efficiently, you have got to sit down beforehand and work it all out in your mind first. I found that even though this was done, yet when the job came to be carried out, some unforeseen problems would arise and have to be solved forthwith.

During my Athlone period, we relaid nearly the whole way from Athlone to Westport and many other parts of the district as well. I should explain that Mr. Bretland, then Chief Engineer of the MGWR, had in 1923, got the approval of his Board to spend money on the establishment of a relaying depot at Mullingar, and the construction of a relaying train, including the famous cantilever, which he had designed in conjunction with the pulley-manufacturing firm of Herbert Morris. This train started working on the Sligo line in 1923, and was only withdrawn during the Second World War due to shortage of materials. Unfortunately while the location of the depot at Mullingar was ideal for the MGWR system, it was not suitable for the GSR system. At a later date, the supervision of the train came under me, and when I tried the experiment of using it on the Mallow-Waterford line. I found it was impossible for the supply train to bring the new track from the depot to the site of the work and the old track back in one day.

Towards the end of the 1920s there was a period of intense financial depression, when it was decided for economic reasons to single the double portions of the Galway line west of Clonsilla and from Mullingar to Multyfarnham. The relaying train was ideal for the lifting and relaying elsewhere of the line to be recovered. One outcome of the period of intense financial depression was a major reorganisation of the Permanent Way Department in 1930. The number of districts was reduced from six to four, and the number of permanent way

inspectors reduced from 60 to 36. The Broadstone and Athlone districts were abolished. As a result I was transferred as assistant to Westland Row. Then I was transferred to Waterford in 1932. This district was very attractive from many points of view. There was very much beautiful country in it, especially the lines from Waterford to Mallow and Limerick, and Dublin via New Ross and Wexford. In addition, Rosslare harbour is a place full of interest, particularly if one is fond of the sea. I remember how much I enjoyed the experience when Foreman Moncas asked me if I would like to go down in a diving suit and have a look at the bottom of the pier. I readily accepted and I'm only sorry now that a camera was not available at the time.

However, time, as it always does, marched on, and in 1936, Mr. Bretland, the then Chief Engineer, retired and Mr. G. Murphy was appointed to succeed him, and I was promoted to the position of his assistant. The next thirteen years saw many changes. At this time the GSR took over a considerable number of private bus and lorry companies as well as the Dublin United Tramway Company. The Permanent Way Department became responsible for the maintenance of bus or lorry depots in the cities and larger towns. What I called 'spacious days' were gone, and we were no longer purely railway men. I ran the department for ten months when Mr. Murphy became ill and retired. In 1949 Mr. Somerville Large was put in charge of the department and I was sent to run the Dublin District. This I found a great relief as I always liked district work.

As I look back on my working life, I am glad to say that I can remember only one regrettable feature and that is that over the last few years, I had to spend so much time on dealing with matters arising out of the closing of branch lines and the lifting of tracks. When I travel through Connemara I felt a real pang of regret as I looked at the places where the railway had been and where I had spent many happy days in my youth. And now after 39 ½ years of working life, I have laid down my gauge, and I can honestly say that I am very glad I spent my time as permanent way engineer.

Chapter 3
Transition to a
Modern Railway

The world of the permanent way was a demanding one in the past. It meant heavy physical labour. Here, in a series of interviews, staff relate how they kept the trains running safely on the track in all weathers and conditions. They tell how mechanisation was gradually introduced and how some of the burden was reduced. In these tales of good humour, mixed with seriousness, we explore a great tradition.

Harold Mc Intyre
Civil Engineer, NIR, retired.

I joined the railway in late 1933. This was as an apprentice engineer in the Great Northern Railway (Ireland). It was during the time of the Great Depression. I went to the district engineer's office in Enniskillen as an unpaid apprentice. An opportunity arose to get paid employment as a timekeeper for the permanent way plus clerical work in the locomotive depot in Clones. I took that job and I was there for four or five years.

I soon settled into the work. My permanent way inspector was very fastidious about his dress and appearance. While most of his contemporaries could best be described as rough diamonds, he on the other hand could have been classed as a cultured pearl! He always walked the track with the wind on his back, carried an umbrella in wet weather, with his track gauge strapped over his shoulder, and wearing overshoes. He made copious notes during his daily travels and he was forever reminding me that 'a bad pencil is better than a good memory.'

My first encounter with a relaying gang proved daunting. It was like the first day at school. There were those large men, clad in rough clothes, throwing sleepers into wagons with abandon, while I was a somewhat overdressed young man in that company, skipping out of the way of sleepers that were deliberately aimed at my feet as I tried to make a count of the sleepers being loaded.

I came back to Enniskillen and the War broke out shortly afterwards. During the Second World War it was very busy. Goods trains at night, troop trains, they were all on the go. Suddenly, the railway was stretched to the limit to cope with the volume of traffic placed on it. Money and materials were made available for large scale renewals. We carried on with relaying every Sunday. Rails came from America. They were bullhead, but it was the hardest steel, very difficult to cut or bore.

There was plenty of work, lots of relaying. The staff in the office consisted of the district engineer, assistant engineer, a clerk, and a typist. It wasn't enough, so I spent most of my time in the district engineer's office as an additional helper. Then, in 1943, I was appointed as assistant to the inspector in Omagh. Omagh was a big district, it ran from Dungannon to Derry. There was plenty of work and that was where I got my permanent way knowledge. As part of my training, I had to spend two very cold winter months sharing the living and working conditions of a mobile relaying gang.

Every six weeks or so the permanent way had to load up a train of locomotive ashes, this was to get rid of it. These were dumped down the sides of banks. Once, it caused a landslide near Portadown, because of the steep angle of repose. On some of the branch lines they used locomotive ash as ballast. It was no use at all, it made for rough permanent way and there were drainage problems.

In 1951 I was transferred to Banbridge as an inspector, third class. Then, as vacancies arose, I moved along and by 1955 I was in Portadown where I was in a senior man's post, from then on until the Ulster Transport Authority (UTA) took us over in 1958. Around 1961 the UTA appointed me as engineer and then I became district engineer. The district was comprised of Belfast to the Border, to Londonderry via Portadown, to Armagh. Lines were closed and eventually I was given the Bangor line to make up for it.

I was glad to retire, because I was working every weekend, and of course you weren't paid for that. There were the budgets, but I always managed to get my relaying programme done. It was all jointed track in my time, but we did the first bit of CWR at the end of my career.

I was looking forward to retirement, I enjoyed my time, but I had felt that I had come to the end of my tether. I retired on the day of my 65th birthday. I didn't wait until the end of the month. Things happened at home; unfortunately my wife was killed in a tragic accident. I was asked to come back. I would have been glad to come back for nothing. It made me up and I started all over again. I was back for six months and later I was back for 19 months.

The Troubles interfered with us. There were bridges being blown up. It held us up terribly badly. There was one bridge at Kilnasaggart, I think it was blown up five times. There was another one between it and the Border; it was blown up one Sunday, and we had it fixed that night again. We just filled it in, it was a little bridge, not used by anybody. Then a hundred people emerged, saying they used it, looking for compensation. So we cleared out the bridge within a few days. The temporary filling was taken away. Previously when an incident occurred we could come in to fix it right away, but the Army put an end to that. They wouldn't let us in for a week, as they said it was too dangerous. But it never was dangerous. The fellows who were blowing up the bridges didn't do it well, the explosion mostly went up in the air. The damage was never too serious. Twelve foot was about the biggest size of the hole that was created. They never were able to close both lines at any time. We used steel waybeams carrying the rails, but with these sitting on the arch it meant the track had to be raised and the approach ramped up.

The GNR (I) was a good company and people had a pride in it, but quite frankly, when we went into the UTA, people were treated better. There was a caste system in the GNR, you had to say 'sir' to people. You didn't have to say 'sir' in the UTA, you were able to call them by their Christian name. The UTA was much more easygoing. In the GNR the Chief Engineer's head office was in Dublin and the district engineers' offices were in Enniskillen and in Belfast.

It was dreadful hard work for the men. The beater packing was hard, two men with those big picks. Every thing was lifted by hand including the rails put on a wagon. When I entered the service, maintenance methods had remained virtually unchanged for more than half a century and in my time I was to see those methods give way to mechanisation.

I joined a steam railway and saw it phased out in favour of diesel. Many people had a genuine affection for steam, but when I recall the battering and the banging of the smoke, grease and grime and the general discomfort, as I made countless footplate journeys, I cannot say that I too regret the passing of steam. It was a common sight in those days to see the permanent way inspector riding the footplate. In fact the drivers insisted in having them there to note track defects, yet those same drivers were not averse to warning gangs along the line that the inspector was walking the track towards them. This they did by bringing their hand up to their cap, a custom carried over from the time that inspectors wore hats and the signal that the 'hat' was on his way was duly noted by the permanent way staff.

An inspector travelling by train once leaned out of the carriage window and threw a bundle of rule books to a gang at the other side of the line. The bundle struck the ganger on the face throwing him down the bank. He complained to the inspector that he might have suffered an injury. The inspector told him that it should be a lesson to him; if he had not been looking at the driver for a signal, he would have seen that he, the inspector was at the carriage window.

I retired on 5th March 1979. I was 95 this year. I'm quite fit, I was always a great walker. No one walked the line more than I did. Finally, we owe a debt to the men along the track whose task is to keep it in safe condition. Throughout most of my long service I was in close contact with trackmen. I drank tea from their black cans, shared their jokes and received much good advice and encouragement but above all else, I had their trust and loyalty.

Tom Young
Mobile Ganger, Athlone, retired. Died May 2009.

I'm 90 years of age. I started on the Great Southern Railway in Kildare in 1941. My first job was a resleepering job from the Curragh into Kildare town. The job was that the ganger laid out ten boxes, ten bays as they called them. This was the stones between the sleepers; you got two hours to take them out. If you had them out sooner you could have a smoke. But if you didn't have the ten out in two hours you were in bother, the other fellows would be gone and you were there. But anyway, I got by. That was my first job, I remember exactly, between the 27¾ to 29¼ miles. I remember we started there the 3rd June 1941 and we completed the job on the 8th November. This was a mile and a half of resleepering. It was bullhead track; we had to break out the bolts. Then the stones came. It was first jacked up and shovel packed and then it was beater packed.

I moved from there then to North Wall. First the Point and then Spencer Dock. They were two very busy depots at that time. All the freight from the West of Ireland was dealt with in Spencer Dock and a lot of the transferred stuff was dealt with in the Point. You had very little time to do work. When you did get possession, you had to get moving. I was there for six months. I did a while in Canal Street. I finished there in May 1942. When I was in Dublin I stayed with an uncle of mine who was a loco driver in Kingsbridge at the time. I cycled from Inchicore to North Wall and used to cycle down the quays across Butt

Bridge and down to the Point. There was no problem cycling in those days. I did enjoy my time in Kildare. I stopped in Kildare town and cycled across the Curragh every morning. I got interested in the horse that time and I saw the stable boys exercising the horses. I nearly lost time watching it, so I came out earlier so I could watch them. It was the real Curragh down all the way into Kildare station, there wasn't a bush, and it's still the same.

I was appointed to a miles gang as a platelayer between Mullingar and Castletown. I was 18 months there and during that time I cycled from home here. It was 14 miles each way. I left there in October 1943 and I got a platelayer's position on the Portarlington branch. That was the Ballycumber-Athlone section. I put in a year there and I came back nearer Athlone. At this time on the Athlone branch there was no such thing as relaying heard tell of. It was during the war years and you were nearly expected to keep it with needle and thread. There was no material, no bolts; it was hard going to keep it. And then at that time traffic was heavy, there were turf trains running to Dublin. Eventually in 1950 there was relaying sanctioned for the Portarlington branch. So I started on that and that was hard work too. You had to use the shovel. All the rails and sleepers you took out had to be loaded, it was hard going, it was all by hand. At that time when you got out the sleepers and rails, the bed then had to be hacked. We got through it and I was appointed a ganger here in 1968. I did ten years as ganger on the Portarlington branch and in 1978, I was appointed mobile ganger in Athlone. During my five years there I lived to see the panel train and all these things.

Now, the time I'm talking about, there was no tea breaks. In the morning you worked from eight to half past 12 and you got whatever you had and you worked again from quarter past one to half five. It was a 48 hour week and from eight to quarter past 12 on Saturdays. My good point was that I had an interest in my job. I always had an interest in it even from the first day I joined it.

The Galway line was single, it was singled in 1932, I think. It was a double line from Broadstone to Ballinasloe and it was a double line from Athlone to Roscommon. Broadstone was closed in January 1937. They reversed the points at Glasnevin, so the west of Ireland trains went to Connolly and Pearse. The Galway main line was Athlone to Mullingar. The switch to Portarlington through here took place in 1973 when the passenger and freight Galway and Westport trains were rerouted through Portarlington.

The Loughrea branch was closed. The West Clare, the Ballinrobe branch; those were closed. They were all closed in my time. Clonsilla to Navan, they were all working when I joined the railway. When the railways were closing down all over the place you were wondering where you were going to go next.

It was hardship, but I have to tell you, I'd be happy to go back and do the same thing again. I enjoyed the permanent way, things didn't go so well sometimes with inspectors and that sort of thing but it all went well. The good thing was if you got in with a group of lads on the job, the crack was going on and it was good.

Right. The workforce poses at the north portal of No. 4 Tunnel on Bray Head, in November 1917, during its construction. The resident engineer, W. H. Hinde, with stick, can be seen to the left of the raised platform. (Derek Paine)

Jim Cregan
Chief Permanent Way Inspector, Limerick Junction, retired.

I was 15 when I joined in 1939. I'm 84 now. I was the tea boy for the relaying gang; I used to boil the cans for them. The relaying ganger had me doing the heavy work as part of the gang, even though I was supposed to be boiling cans. At that age, all that bothered me was hurling. Balingrane was where I started on the Foynes branch, that's where I'm from. On the relaying gang in 1940 the take home pay was two pounds six and five pence per week. I worked for the county council then as I was too young.

Then I went back to the railway. We used to get a few months on the railway then, weeding. I went from that and got a job, as a man then, you could say. I joined a relaying gang then. There were no expenses, it was hard work. They'd nearly want you to carry two sleepers at the time. They worked all over the place. I travelled around with them. I walked every bit of the Limerick Area at that time, which was from the Devon Road on the North Kerry line down to Westport.

John Hyde Ffolliott was the district engineer when I started. I was there for four years with the relaying gang. There was a vacancy for a ganger in Limerick yard. There were three gangs then. There was the No. 1, the No. 2 and the road gangs. Limerick was a very big yard then. I got appointed and I used to relieve the inspectors then, all of them.

One time, a lot went to Cardiff for the Permanent Way Institution. I didn't go at all. John Hyde sent for me. I was only a rookie inside in the gang. He knew me. He said: 'I'm doing a bit of relaying down in the Ballina branch, I want you to go down and take charge of it.' If a hole had opened up in front of me, I'd have fallen into it. I never expected it, especially as the chief inspector normally did that job. So it was he who set me going, John Hyde; I got on great with him. It was very hard to put a name on him, because he was called everything. He was very straight. Hyde Ffolliott was a gentleman. He used to wear plus fours with long stockings on the railway. They were organising some form of party for retirement. They were saying, what will we have. 'Biscuits and lemonade' was what he said. I couldn't say one bad word about him; it was he who put me out. He gave me my start.

There were exams for inspectors. The Chief Engineer set these. I had to go up to Dublin. There was no training, you were expected to know. You were a ganger, and you went up. You had the written exam and, after lunch, an interview. I went to the interview and there were five engineers. There was the district engineer for where the vacancy was. There was the Chief Engineer, the assistant chief engineer and the personnel officer. That morning, you'd be working with a pick and shovel. And you'd be terrified that you'd make a hames of yourself. The first question he asked me was how much would it cost to lay a mile of track. How would I know that? That was a stupid question to ask a rookie.

I was made inspector in 1964 in Sligo. I went from Sligo then to Nenagh. When I was living in Sligo. I'd get off the train in Ballymote and walk into Boyle. I think it was 14 miles. You had all day to do it. You'd take the bus home. You wouldn't be home till eight o'clock, but you wouldn't care if you'd have it done for another while.

I never got Ballinamore inspector's division. It was a stepping stone for everyone. It had been done away with in my time. John Downey said it had a dote of a narrow gauge, dotes of level crossings and a little train set. Every one of the inspectors appointed there, the first vacancy anywhere else, you were made – you got the job. They used only go down there for a holiday, it was a like a rest period before the bigger jobs.

I cycled on a rail bike. The inspector, the sweat would be running down him pedalling. The chief would only be going through the motions. Sometimes you'd get the staff, if there was nothing doing with the trains. The rail bikes were light. You could hop off and grab them in the middle if the train was coming. I got a couple of quare frights with them. If it was wild at all you wouldn't hear the train. Sometimes engineers went on the bikes but they wouldn't be pedalling, they'd be writing away on their notes.

I was made chief in the then Divisional Engineer Gerry Dalton's time. I retired in 1990. There was no mobile phone or computers then. It was all letters and it worked. My letters were short. I had the advantage that I appointed nearly all my own inspectors. I was able to choose the fellow I wanted. You'd know anyhow. I was 44 years altogether, I enjoyed it all but it was rough. Funny, I didn't miss it. It was bred into me, but when I left it I never went near it.

Right. The view from the Inspection Car as it passes over the Boyne Viaduct, June 2009. From left: Divisional Engineer Brian Lucas, Inspector Peter Bannon and Assistant Divisional Engineer Colin Hedderly observe while Seamus Kenny drives.

J.J. Maxwell
Permanent Way Inspector, Navan, retired.

I joined the railway on the 12th December 1945. I was appointed ganger in 1949. I joined in Roscrea and was then transferred to Cloughjordan when my father retired. He was a ganger in the railway, and his father, and my son is working in the railway. So there are four generations of Maxwells in the railway. I was ganger in Roscrea for years and years. It was in the 1960s that I put in a railway to the Silvermines. We had 12 lorries drawing stuff and there were 2000 tonnes of filling brought into the Silvermines site to build up the line. I got a phone call one day to collect an engineer at the station in Nenagh. I sent in a lorry to collect him. He introduced himself as David Berkery. 'JJ', he said, 'I'm a junior engineer and I know nothing about a railway.' I said 'You're the most honest engineer I've met, because we all have to learn. If you give me versines and curvatures and all that, you don't have to worry, I'll look after that and put in the track.'

Anyway, time passed. There was a vacancy for an inspector in Tuam. I applied for it. Larry Stephens who was a chief inspector in Limerick told me: 'You're a cert.' Well, I wasn't, someone else got it. After a while I applied for Navan. I got Navan and transferred there in 1969. It was a thing I never regretted. My children went to school in Trim. They all got jobs, thanks be to God, with not a bother on them.

There was 20 miles to Kingscourt and every bit of fencing on either side was falling down. No matter what you did, unless you renewed it, you couldn't

Right. At York Road in Belfast around 1905: an Allday and Onions Motorised Inspection Vehicle. The Chief Civil Engineer of the Northern Counties Committee Railway, Berkeley Deane Wise, is at the front right. (Ulster Folk & Transport Museum)

maintain. It was heartbreak. In those days there was no money. I remember when I came here we pulled out sleepers and turned them upside down, just to get a drill hole. We used to call this shoving through the house. You'd 18 inches outside the rail on each side. You'd take out the screws, you'd get a bar and you'd push the sleeper through so that you could redrill and refix the rails, all to try and keep the gauge. We maintained here on shoelaces. It was terrible, because I had marvellous track in Limerick. That was the Limerick to Ballybrophy branch practically new, all relaid with 90 lb bullhead track and then when I came here and saw what was here, I nearly fainted and said: 'What in the name of God drove me here at all?' We were getting second hand sleepers on the Navan branch that would only last five years. I even marked them, and after five years I was pulling them out. I asked that they would send a second hand sleeper that would last at least ten years. It was false economy.

The greatest boost we ever got was when they started the DART. We got the Dublin Suburban stuff all the way down the Kingscourt line. We didn't know ourselves. They'd take them up on a Sunday and load them up. We'd get them on a Tuesday. The gypsum train to Kingscourt would be cancelled on a Tuesday and we'd have a full day, and we'd get a half a mile in, using the Donellis. We threw out the old rails for the gantry rails of the Donellis. All we did with the old sleepers was fire them down the bank. They were completely rotten, no man would buy them. The track from Dublin was the best thing that ever happened.

Johnny Shalvey was the ganger at the time. He was an old timer who wouldn't stand for any codology. And the engineer, Mr Yates, in his own way, was a gentleman. He came down this day, in the inspection car, with Dinny Redmond. And Shalvey had his work prepared and everything was right, and Mr Yates said: 'Ganger Shalvey, how are things going? 'Not so well, Mr. Yates', he said. 'Why?' 'This so and so place is falling apart and there will be a terrible accident.' And he went along and took out the spikes out of eleven or twelve sleepers. 'That's what we are dealing with now, Mr Yates'. He had them already loosened. Mr. Yates nearly died.

There were great characters, but I often wonder, when I joined the railway in 1945, 90 percent of the people who worked on the railway couldn't write. I spent three years in a technical school. I was able to read the ruler backways. When we were building crossovers and turnouts and them sorts of thing, I was able to read the distances between holes in the stock rails and things like that. They used to say, he's a chancer, and they wouldn't believe I was able to do it. They had little sticks, I think the first was four and the next was 21 inches, and so on. They had these sticks cut out and that's how they were able to measure. They weren't able to read numbers. You'd say to a fellow: 'Would you take charge of a bridge painting gang?' He'd agree. Then I'd say: 'Wait now, I'll get you a time-keeping book.' Oh no, end of story. Even though he was a most capable man, you could trust him with your life, but he hadn't the education.

I met some great characters. I was in Navan up to 1990 and I enjoyed the best of health. I'm now 83 and I feel better than when I retired. Times were good and CIÉ was good to me.

Tom O' Donnell
Permanent Way Inspector, Dundalk, retired.

I joined the railway in July 1947. I was nearly 20 years of age. I joined Cannon's gang. It was down in Athenry, where I came from. He was relaying close to my, which was near the railway. There were 12 in a gang. We did resleepering there first, and then the chief inspector at the time, Looney, asked me if I would go in the relaying gang. We travelled around the entire Limerick District. At that time the Limerick District went down to Sligo, up to Athlone, down to Westport, Ballina and Galway. It went down to the border with Kerry, but it didn't go to Limerick Junction. So we left Athenry and went down to Ballyvarry, down in Mayo. Then we went to Limerick to do a job at the end of 1950. There was a vacancy there and I got appointed as a platelayer in Limerick. I worked in Limerick until 1953 and then I started relaying in a gang of my own. I travelled to every part of the district. Then around 1957 I got appointed ganger outside Limerick, between Boher and Drumkeel. I lifted the Ballinrobe Line between Ballinrobe and Claremorris. Then I lifted the West Clare railway in 1960 and I lifted the line from Birr down to Roscrea. When we lifted the West Clare, it was nearly all pulled by hand. Then we got a winch, it was handy enough. There was an inspector that time from Limerick; he was a great man to invent things. He was a very handy fellow, but the poor chap died suddenly after. He'd be always out and never let you down. He'd always be able to repair something, There was only six of us. There was a man behind us selling the sleepers. Even on the Ballinrobe line we sold every one. They were six feet and they were suitable for anything like fencing. You couldn't lift the line fast enough. There were some good rails. Some went for replacement, some went for scrap. We sent some out foreign to some of the railways. It was light poundage. We left the bridges alone. They were left there. That was the end of the history of the West Clare, 'Are you right there Michael, are you right?' It was 52 miles down to Moyasta Junction. Then there was one line into Kilkee and another into Kilrush. It must have been over 60 miles. It didn't take too long, just a bit over a year. We had two engines working; they were wee diesel railcars that pulled the wagons. We could only load two wagons at a time. The engine went back out and we used the winch to pull up the rails.

I was a traffic guard as well. I had a guard's certificate. They were short of guards and sometimes I'd go as a guard on a special down to Tuam or other specials. I was happy, because the run to Tuam was four o'clock in the evening and there was overtime, you wouldn't be down to Tuam until eight or nine o'clock at night. And then there'd be a special starting off at four o'clock in the morning. It was good.

I got appointed as permanent way inspector in Navan in 1963. I spent a year in Navan, and then a vacancy came in Dundalk. I went down there and was there since. When I started first there was no machinery. Resleepering, boring or cutting rails, it was all by hand. It was slow work, but it was still done. Crossovers were built; you skidded them in, and you had no crane.

During the Troubles they never blew up our side of the Border. The northern crowd blew up just at the Border. There were engines blown up and they had to have buses. There was lots of trouble for the traffic people. Anytime there was blowing up, I'd have to walk the line with the police. It was mostly Sunday evenings that they'd have a false alarm. I'd be out working all day from six o'clock in the morning and then I'd get a call when I'd be having the dinner. Then I'd have to walk the six miles down to the Border. It could be a false alarm. I'm telling you, you'd have to be in good form. And the squad car would carry you in.

The line here was well built. It was the Great Northern Railway; it had a good name. The Irish North was closed in 1958 and men were moved. Some retired, but some had to move house and come and work in Dundalk or Drogheda. There were big closures in the GNR in the fifties. Then the Dundalk works closed in 1958 – that was a great place. They say there were tradesmen there that could do anything. Some of the men I had, they were out on the lines that were closed. They were able to go home to their own place, they hadn't to change residence.

When we got the first tamper, it was a real crude thing; you'd have to have jacks in front of it. Still, it's getting better all the time. Lord, the beater packing in the old days was terrible, sleeper after sleeper. You'd be wondering when would it end. It was a good hard life, but then I was young and enjoyed it. I enjoyed my time as an inspector. I had good staff, they're still good.

Denis Redmond

Chief Permanent Way Inspector, Dublin, retired.

I joined the permanent way in 1947. It was just shortly after the Second World War. Nothing much had been done during the war as materials couldn't be obtained. There had been no rails or sleepers imported and there was a big backlog of work to be done. It was just keeping things alive, such as reconditioning old bolts, cleaning the threads. They introduced a lot of native timber for sleepers, beech and oak. They lasted a very short time as fungus grew on them very quickly. They only lasted a few years, even the oak. Immediately after the war, they brought in Oregon pine. The life of these was short also, about ten or 15 years. Then the French maritime pine was introduced in the early 50s, I think we are still buying some of that. It's mainly concrete sleepers now, with hardwood for points and crossings.

I remember that I started on plain track near Bray, working on cleaning out stone ballast. It was hack and shovel work. Everything was measured. There would be about 20 in the gang that time. Each man would get about eight boxes (sleeper spaces). All lined up, you'd cover a lot of ground with 20 men. As the last man would finish, he'd move to the front. They'd be moving around all the time. They used to call it 'hind man up'. They did 16 before lunch and 16 after, 32 boxes in a day.

The working hours were a 48 hour week, from eight in the morning until half past five, with three quarters of an hour for lunch. I often heard fellows talking about when, back in the 1920s, they had to work a 12 hour day. I remember the old fellows talking about it, going out to walk the road at six o'clock on a winter's morning with an oil hand lamp.

Manpower was plentiful and cheap at the time. A lot of the lads were demobbed out of the Irish Army. When I started, the wages were three pounds two and six per week. That was the A rate. The A rate applied to cities and large towns; the smaller towns would be the B rate; the country areas would have the C rate. It was strange, Bray carried the A rate and Foxrock had a C rate.

There was great camaraderie on the job then. Very little Sunday work, you could do most of the work in between trains. It was hand work; you didn't have to bring in machines. There'd be a speed restriction of course. The ganger would have an understanding with the signalman that he'd be breaking the road at certain times during the day. He wouldn't be talking to him every time he'd start the work. He'd be four or five miles away. The fastest transport was the bicycle. You depended on the weekly circular to see if there were any extra special trains. The ganger would know on the day that these were coming. If there was nothing in the circular, nothing was coming in between the regular trains. If something had to run as a special that wasn't programmed, they used a system; the previous train would have two tail lamps on it or a red disk with a red flag. The staff would be watching for this on passing trains. It worked. I never heard tell of trains being blocked. Everything was local at that time and the ganger was the head man. He had more power than even the inspector over his area. The inspector wouldn't interfere with him as things were usually in order.

There was no weed spraying during the war, and it didn't come back for a long time after. During the growth season the track had to be hand weeded. Between late April and July, on every length, an extra man would have to be taken on. That's all the gang would do for a couple of months, the whole of them weeding. They'd use the hack, loosen up the ballast and pull the weeds out of it. It would have to be done a couple of times. Often there were times when you'd have done a mile or so and you'd see them growing again.

The mechanisation came in around 1950. We had a Chief Engineer at the time, Mr Dan Herlihy, who introduced this. It had been the same pattern of work, when I started, as had been going on for the previous hundred years. There were no machines for doing even the simplest tasks such as cutting and boring rails and boring sleepers. It took about an hour to cut a rail using a hacksaw. Sleepers were bored using a hand auger. We then got in a small machine that could cut, bore rails and timber called the 'John Bull'. There was also a Matisa rail drill.

Up to then, packing the track had been done by a technique called beater packing. The beater was a pick with one end for beating the stones. The ganger would have a man with a track jack who would lift and level the track. One man would beater pack a sleeper to hold a lift. The ganger would go along one rail for three or four rail lengths with the gang packing behind the sleeper ends.

Then they would return on the other rail. And then it changed. I remember the first tamper coming in, it was four-wheeled and two-axle, made by Matisa. You had to level the track ahead of the tamper. It only tamped but this was a great improvement. It was very noisy. It was self propelled with a mechanical squeeze, no hydraulics. It was a short machine, with the operator in a small cab. In fact, I saw one when I was out in Mozambique. It was in on a siding. The Portuguese must have had one there during their time.

We graduated from hand relaying to mechanical relaying using agricultural tractors in the 1950s and this was used a lot. Three tractors were employed. Slings were attached to the hydraulics at the back of a tractor to lift out the old sleepers. A second tractor was used to scarify the ballast. The third lifted in the new sleepers. The rails were lifted in by hand using hand barrows. This system did away with a lot of the hard manual work.

When I started on the DSE, that was a busy track between Bray and Dublin. Any major work had to be done at night. You had morning peaks and evening peaks. Between Bray and Shanganagh Junction you had the Harcourt Street line. There'd be a train out of Bray every 15 minutes, one to Harcourt Street and maybe two to Westland Row. It would be busy from seven up to around half nine. Then it would be slack, maybe one every hour after that, until four in the evening, then it would be getting busy out of town. There'd be extra trains at lunch hour. People would go home for lunch. Maybe one out of Westland Row and one out of Harcourt Street. People would be going down as far as Dundrum or Foxrock, from Harcourt Street, and the same as far as Blackrock or Dún Laoghaire, out of Westland Row, for their lunch. There used to be a system on the Westland Row line in those days, all your trains wouldn't work from Bray into Westland Row. There'd be special ones. In peak periods, a train would leave from Bray, stop at Shankill, Killiney and Dalkey and run as an express after that. A train in the siding in Dalkey would pull in behind it and pick up the other stations after that. There'd be more trains in near Dublin. It was very well organised. Never many problems. Then you had trains going to the pier for the boat in Dún Laoghaire. You'd have two trains from there to Westland Row and one to Kingsbridge, up around Cabra and through the Phoenix Park tunnel.

The track was good; it was mainly 85 lb bullhead rail. It seemed to always run smoothly, steam engines then of course. They had the bunker steam engines on the DSE. The coal was in a coal box attached to the loco, there was no tender. We had an electric train during the war on the Harcourt Street line: the Drumm battery train. It ran until about 1948. They'd be charged at night, one at Bray and the other at Harcourt Street.

There was no special training in health and safety in those days. There were no hard hats, visibility vests. boots or gloves. If there was an accident, an accident form had to be filled in. The cause of the accident had to be explained by ticking off certain boxes. For example was it caused by negligence on the injured man's part or was it faulty tools or equipment etc? One box was down for 'misadventure.' This box was always ticked.

I came into Dublin in 1952 and I got involved in the yard relaying. We relaid all the station yards, both freight and passenger, in the Dublin district. The yards like North Wall and Kingsbridge were marshalling yards and very busy. We were only able to do the major work on Sundays.

It was Dublin District in those days. In 1960 it became Dublin Area. Somerville Large had been district engineer and then Plumer came in the 1950s. Somerville Large was well-known everywhere. Gatekeepers and all, they all knew him. He made his presence felt. I remember one day, I was doing relief inspector on the DSE in Bray. The Dublin inspector's division went to Avoca at that time. We were in the inspection car coming up. It happened that there was a farmer exercising horses along the Murrough. Out of Newcastle and by Five Mile Point, there's a nice grassy area there. This is on the sea side and is apparently railway property. Large stopped the car. 'Redmond', he said, he never called you by your Christian name, 'Who's that fellow trespassing in there?' And I knew him, 'Mr. Mannion', I said, 'a big horsy farmer.' 'Go over and tell him to remove himself, he has no right to be there.' So I went over and I said to the man: 'The Chief Engineer, Mr. Large, is with us and he says you are trespassing, and you have to get that horse out of here.' 'Large, I've heard of that man's name, Somerville?' 'Yes', says I. 'I've heard of that fellow, I'll talk to him', and he rode up and stuck the head of the horse into the inspection car. 'Which of you is Large?', he said. There was the chief inspector, the inspection car driver, myself and Large. 'I'm Mr. Large.' 'I'm Mr. Mannion, Large', he says. 'My grandfather exercised horses here. My father exercised horses here and I'm going to damn well exercise horses here whether you like it or not.' Large, he cooled down. He didn't say anything. We didn't hear anything about it afterwards.

Track alignment bothered him a lot for years. He always had gangs pulling at it. They had track liners. When you pulled the handle it would lift and slide the track. He didn't think they were doing enough at it and he sent out a circular to all inspectors and maintenance gangers. On Monday, the gang was to do nothing but line up the track. One morning he was down in the inspection car at Newcastle, near the same place we had talked about. He knew every ganger, of course. Phil Leonard was fencing on a Monday. Large was travelling along in the inspection car and he saw the gang repairing the fence, so he stopped. 'Leonard, why aren't you lining the track, this is Monday?', he says. 'I have to fence these animals out, Mr. Large.' 'Didn't you get my circular?', he says. 'I did Mr. Large, you should have sent one to that white-headed fellow out in the field.'

Mr. Large's bark was worse than his bite. He'd be very blunt and kind of frighten you. After all though, he never took any drastic action against a fellow, he just told you what he thought of you, there and then and that was it. He was a good engineer, to be able to maintain a railway out of scrap.

As I said, from 1952 I was mostly engaged in renewing points and crossings in the Dublin District. Then in 1959 I went to be inspector in Navan. I only did six months up there. I remember, I had got married in June and went there and went back in December, to Liffey Junction, on the Midland. The Liffey Junction inspector's division was between North Wall and on the North Wall

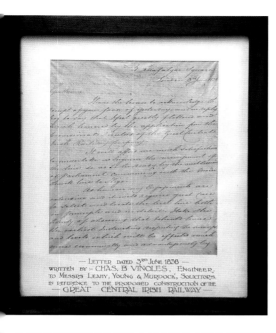

— LETTER DATED 3RD JUNE 1838 —
WRITTEN BY ─ CHAS. B VIGNOLES, ENGINEER,
TO MESSRS LEAHY, YOUNG & MURDOCK, SOLICITORS,
IN REFERENCE TO THE PROPOSED CONSTRUCTION OF THE
─ GREAT CENTRAL IRISH RAILWAY ─

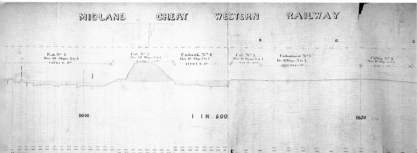

MIDLAND GREAT WESTERN RAILWAY

1 IN 600

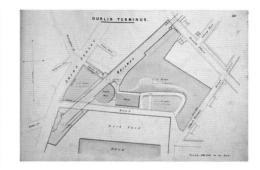

DUBLIN TERMINUS.

Midland up to Glasnevin Junction and down as far as Killucan. I was a couple of years there. The inspection car coming in your area was a big event, especially with Mr. Large coming. There was always a problem with that line. Large was always complaining about it. We did a lot of relaying. I think it was around 1963 when Large came down and inspected it. At the end, he hadn't much to say. 'The division is looking very well, Redmond', he said. I was speechless. I never thought he'd say that even if it was so. And Bill O' Keefe (chief inspector, in Dublin) said to me: 'You can sleep all day now. I never heard Large say that before, he must be going a bit deaf or something'. I worked hard there for the five years I was there. It was tough going, we did an awful lot of relaying, reballasting and realignment.

A vacancy came up in Cork for a chief inspector and Bill O' Keefe (who was a Corkman) asked me to apply. I wasn't even dreaming of that. I said: 'What would I be going down to Cork for and I wouldn't even get it if I applied for it.' He said: 'You should apply.' I discussed it with my wife and she said that it was up to me. We'd be moving house for maybe a tenner a week in my wages. In fact I think it cost me more to rent the house in Cork than the one in Dublin. There was a portion of that tenner gone. People advised me to go down, so I chanced it.

I went to Cork and was a couple of years there. I liked Cork. There are all the same facilities in the city as in Dublin, but it was at a much more relaxed pace. The area was far less busy than Dublin was. We had the main line from Charleville to Cobh. We had the Youghal branch. We had the Mallow-Tralee into Killarney and down to Tralee and onto Farranfore. The North Kerry was open as well as the Fenit branch and Castleisland. There was the Mallow-Waterford line. That was a very scenic route, down along the Blackwater. It made for a very enjoyable trip in the inspection car on a summer's morning.

They were lifting the Cork and Bandon at that time. They were up as far as Bandon and I went out, there was trouble with the stocks or something. I had to go out and investigate. I remember walking out and I remember the Ballinhassig and the Chetwynd viaducts. They were a fierce height and there was decking missing. I remember being very nervous walking across them. Chetwynd was the one where this famous bowler, Barry was his name, lofted the bowl over it. I went out as far as Bandon, but I knew from Bill O' Keefe, my old colleague, who knew all the area, that down around Clonakilty and West Cork there was beautiful country around there.

The chief inspector in Dublin got sick. Mr. O' Connell, who was area engineer in Cork at that time, said to me: 'Bill O' Keefe has gone sick and Mr. Yates wants to know would you go up and relieve'. Yates was area engineer in Dublin, he took over from Plumer in 1960.

Bill O' Keefe subsequently died and the position became vacant. I hadn't put in an application. My wife had said, 'Please yourself, I'm happy enough here in Cork.' Yates said to me: 'I don't see your application in for the job here.' I said: 'I can't get a house, Mr. Yates.' There was a clamp down with the Building Societies and the Banks at that time, you couldn't get a loan. He said: 'There's a house in

Inchicore'. I said that I had enquired there, there was nothing. 'I'll look into that', he said. So he called me in two days and said: 'There's a house in Inchicore for you.' They were all railway houses. They were old houses, dark, but were sound and dry. But I wanted my own house, the first chance I'd get. I was a year there and I came out to my house here then.

I became chief inspector in Dublin in 1967. Mr. Gill was Chief Civil Engineer. He purchased a few miles of new 60 foot 87 lb bullhead rails to replace a considerable amount of 87 lb 1905 rails on the Cork line. He also purchased a large amount of second-hand flat-bottomed rail from British Rail which had been lifted as a result of the Beeching cuts. These were exceptionally good rails. Then we had a test strip for CWR at Hazelhatch from the 11¼ to the 12½ milepost, called the 'Golden Mile'. Roughly half was made up of concrete sleepers with 92 lb flat-bottom rail; the other half had second-hand timber sleepers with second-hand 87 lb bullhead rail. The rails were assembled and welded at Gormanstown; there was a suitable long bank up there. This was the first time these long welded rails were transported by rail back to Hazelhatch; it took over four rail trucks. It went around curves, and even passed by Islandbridge where there was a sharp curve of 150 m radius. We pulled them off at the site. This was all new to us at the time. We put in the concrete sleepers in panels using the steam crane. The whole exercise went on for six weeks. The old 87 lb rail behaved perfectly and never went out of alignment. Then it was decided to relay with block relaying, with possession of one track at a time. We put in concrete sleepers from Portlaoise. We had no Donellis then and used a Priestman crane. A half a mile on a Sunday. Then there was the CTC project on the Cork line and we had to alter all the yards. Then the mechanical relaying came in, with Donellis. It went like clockwork from the start.

There were many derailments in yards with loose-coupled trains, but that's all gone now. There was a derailment down in Hazelhatch once. I went down to check it out. Mr. Yates was my boss, so I rang him at home, I wanted to tell him what was going on. Mrs. Yates answered. I said that I was looking for Mr. Yates. 'He's not in, Denis', she said. 'Sorry to disturb you, Mrs Yates, but we had a derailment in Hazelhatch and you might tell him'. 'How many fishplates are broken?' she said. 'Oh, you know what I'm talking about, so you can tell him everything is alright, and the road is open now.'

Arthur Plumer, who was a district engineer, was a very humorous man, and was chairman of the Permanent Way Institution for a long time. Plumer once gave a paper where he told the story that the Operating Department rang Somerville Large once to get the exact length of the platform at Blackrock, urgently. As there were no technical staff available at the time, Mr Large rang the ganger and told him that he was sending the office messenger to Blackrock with a measuring tape and would he kindly measure the up platform for him, between the ramps. The ganger sent a note back with the messenger which said: 'Sorry Mr. Large, I wasn't able to measure the platform, the tape wasn't long enough'.

In my time, gangs kept the track well, there were no machines. We had a great quality of gangers, they were great men. They were quite capable of doing their stocks and timesheets properly. Very sound, commonsense guys they were. On the whole, they came up in the hard times. Men would spend years in the relaying gang and would apply for platelayer's positions as they arose. And then you were appointed to the length gang. This wouldn't be as heavy type of work.

Mr. Waters was divisional engineer in the late 1970s. I remember him coming to me one time and telling me, this suburban project was coming and we would have to manage it in-house. I said: 'No way, we'd never cope with it and do divisional maintenance as well.' This project was like building a new railway. About two weeks later he came along and told me: 'It's going to be a special job, I've been promoted to assistant chief civil engineer to look after it.' I said: 'Congratulations, sorry to lose you.' A nice man, Mr. Waters, great to work with. So he set up a special section. He asked me: 'Can you recommend a permanent way inspector? I need one for a start at least.' I said: 'Let me think about that,' and a couple of days after I said: 'Yes, I recommend one fellow. I don't know would he do it or not, he's down in Wexford, I haven't been talking to him. I'd recommend Dan Donovan.' I hadn't known him long. We had only taken over the Waterford area and I had seen a couple of jobs that he had done. But I knew that he was capable of the task. He turned out to be a great success. There was no one who could do it better.

After retiring I went to Mozambique on a consultancy assignment to a railway project there. I spent 15 months there and found it very satisfying. The engineer was Joe Strachan, a Scottish man. We got to know the Mozambican inspectors, including the chief inspector. It was the Beira line up to Machinpanda on the Zimbabwean border. The workers in the railway there were ok, they were capable men. They had two 07 Plasser tampers which were out of commission but we got them back working again. They had a ballast quarry but the machinery in it was in poor condition. We lived in the compound in Beira, which was very comfortable. A one-bedroom flat with a bedroom, kitchen and bathroom, it was ideal. The canteen was right beside us. You couldn't pay cash, you bought a book of coupons for US dollars. It would do a week, a meal and a couple of bottles of beer. Sometimes we'd stop out, up the line in the railway rest houses. Machinpanda was one, Shumaya was another. They were clean. You got your breakfast, fried eggs and chips.

I must say I enjoyed it, it was the best thing I ever did. I didn't go for the sake of the money, it was for the adventure of it. It was a third world country with children going around in their bare feet. It reminded me of Ireland in the thirties. Of course, we had worse weather: at least they have a good climate.

I was down the Rosslare line on the inspection car recently; it was in great condition. All that money invested is now paying dividends. When you look at it in the long term, it's justified. There's nothing to do on that line now, except a bit of tamping. All the yards are top standard points and crossings, I couldn't believe it, the improvement. The standard of the track has improved hundreds of percent, whereas in my day we had to live with very poor materials.

Peter Mc Morrough

Regional Maintenance Executive (Civil), Galway, retired.

I was born in 1928 and joined the railway on the 10th May 1948 as an apprentice. I was interviewed by Mr Somerville Large, district engineer, in Westland Row and sat an exam in the clerical office there, in Mathematics, English and Drawing. Three days afterwards I got a letter saying that I had been successful and that I would start in Westland Row for ten shillings a week, rising to 15 shillings in my second year and one pound a week in my third year.

I was still an apprentice. Later on, we were re-railing on Bray Head. I had been asked by Arthur Plumer, the newly-appointed district engineer, to keep track of progress. The next thing, who descended on the scene but his daughter, June. She happened to be down in Bray, and went up the cliff walk to call in and see her father. He was annoyed, he said she could be in danger. He said: 'You'll have to go.' He called John Troy, the chief inspector and said: 'Troy, have you anyone who could bring this young lady down?' Then he looked at me and said: 'Hold on there, Mc Morrough, you take my daughter down.' Troy said to me: 'Take the rail bike.' There was a double-saddled rail bike there. She sat on one side and I sat on the other. I didn't have to pedal much as we were on the incline. She was delighted at first to be up on a rail bike. The next thing the bike got out of control after about a quarter of a mile. The brake was a leather band around the axle at the back. There was smoke coming out. It was fixed wheel and you'd have to brake by back pedalling and applying the handbrake which was impossible due to our rate of descent. We went down that hill and around the curve at the bottom. Fortunately the signalman was looking up and he opened the gates at the head of the platform at Bray. We went through the gates and we didn't stop until we got to Woodbrook. We walked back to Bray station. If we had hit a set of points wrongly, we'd have been derailed.

In due course I went to Waterford as a draughtsman at £250 a year. I was under Jack Meleady, district engineer. Joe Sullivan was the chief draughtsman. Kerry Brady was the assistant district engineer. I got involved there in all sorts of track maintenance. Also in the soundings at Rosslare harbour, before and after the dredging. I went there from November 1951. I think I left in May 1954 to go to Cork. Thomas Harman was the district engineer there.

Before I left Waterford, I was engaged in time and motion observations of the Matisa packer working on the Waterford-Clonmel line, which was under the control of Ted Glancy, assistant engineer. It was subject to incessant visits from Dan Herlihy, the Chief Engineer. He even pulled in one Sunday evening, going to Ring College with his son on a scholarship. He put the son behind a plate of soup in a hotel while he came up the railway to find out where we were. He asked Ted Glancy what were his observations on this. Ted put his hand in his pocket and took out a cigarette packet with notes written. Herlihy snapped: 'Forget the cigarette packet Glancy, it's in your head it should be.'

Amongst other things I did in Cork, was the disposal of property on the abandonment of railway lines. I was involved in the Schull and Skibereen, the Cork and Macroom, the Farranfore and Valentia, the Tralee and Dingle, the Fermoy and Mitchelstown. Cork was a wonderful place. Tommy Harman was different from the previous engineers I worked with. He was brilliant but he brooked no slackness. There was a series of bells which called you. If you went in and it was a sociable call, he'd just hand you a file; he'd be tapping the heel of a pencil slowly. But if he was on fire, he'd be flipping up the pencil and be hitting it hard. Then he'd let fly.

Dan Herlihy brought Commandant Joe Doyle into CIÉ. Commandant Doyle had been in the Army Engineering Corps looking after demolition of such things as bridges. Joe worked subsequently in CIÉ for a good number of years, blowing up bridges that were derelict. Once there was a project to construct a car park in Parknasilla for the hotel there. There was a rock outcrop inside in the woods. It was planned to cut down the trees, blow out the outcrop and you'd get space for 40 cars. I brought Joe down and he looked at it and said tell me when you are ready to go. He asked did I know anyone in the Army Barracks. I said I didn't know. I found out that he wanted to borrow a plunger and cable. We went up to the Barracks and he got that sorted out.

I used to go with Joe when he was blasting. We used to have two cars, one with the gelignite, which we picked up from a supplier near Ovens in Cork; we had got a licence for it. The detonators went in a separate car. We'd go up to the Barracks and draw the plunger and other things. Joe was in civvies, but when we walked in we'd all get salutes. Joe drove a special car, with a special boot for the gelignite. I drove the staff car.

The day we had planned for Parknasilla, we got a call that Joe couldn't come. I had everything set up. Harman got annoyed. An engineer in the office said:

'Mr. Harman, I'll do it.' Harman asked: 'What experience have you?' 'I studied demolition in college and I also have accompanied Commandant Doyle.' Harman replied: 'Well, I'll ask Large.' Incidentally, they called each other by their Christian names, but everyone else was known by their surnames. 'Well, Paddy, Commandant Doyle is unable to come down to proceed with the demolition for that car park at Parknasilla. My assistant district engineer here said he is competent to do it.' 'Proceed if you are happy', said Large.

So we went down. Joe Doyle had drilled down into the rock. He wanted to shatter rather than explode. The engineer said we'd be all day at this. He ordered eight holes drilled in sideways. He was very professional in ramming in the charges and setting up everything. All guests in the hotel were warned. There was the cry of 'Clear the site'. Then there was this unmerciful explosion and all we could see was this cap of rock going up about 20 feet in the air.

We got the fright of our lives. Afterwards we went round to pick up the two cars at the back of the hotel. The roof of the engineer's car (the one with the reinforced boot) was pushed down – a big rock had blown over the hotel roof and came down on the car. We ended up getting two milesmen with a crowbar who pushed it up so that he could sit comfortably. He drove the car back to Cork.

I went with Joe Doyle and we blew bridges on abandoned lines. This was where it was safe and where it would be difficult to dismantle the bridge; they were mainly steel and timber. One time on Bantry pier, the line was being closed. There was a single track going out to the pier. There were big timber stanchions, two foot square, supporting it. The pier wasn't suitable for the Bantry fishermen. There was no decking, only the track, and they wanted it taken away. Commandant Doyle waited until low tide. There were 18 of these stanchions. He put what he called a necklace around the stanchion and interconnected them. When he pressed the plunger, he blew it at full tide. All you saw was a gurgle of water coming up. We didn't think it was blown at all. What he was doing was ensuring that there was just sufficient charge to cut across each. Then he hitched two fishing boats to the pier with hawsers and the whole thing was pulled out like a big raft. It was a very neat job.

I went from there to Galway in 1960. The office was established there. I worked there with the engineers, Gerry Cleary and Denis Buckley. In Galway we had to look after the railway and we had to look after the hotels, bus garages, as well as the abandoned railway lines. We had to take over the Donegal railways in 1964. All the railways there had ceased in 1959. When the GNR (I) had closed in 1959, that's what crippled them, because the Donegal railways and all the railways up along there were connected into and depended on what was ferried by the GNR. I worked for a while on the Bundoran line, disposing of the track on both sides of the Border. I'd have to go and tell the guards in Bundoran and the police in Pettigo that I'd be crossing over the border. The lifting of the track was done by a contractor. In the end I received a letter from Liam St John Devlin, Chairman of CIÉ, expressing appreciation for my work on the Donegal railways. I stayed based in the Galway office and retired from there in 1992.

Dan Donovan

Permanent Way Inspector, Wexford, retired.

I joined the railway in August 1948. I came in with the traffic people. I was
paid off after four years; they did away with the job. Eventually I joined the
permanent way. My father before me had been a ganger. He had been working
near Mountrath on the Dublin-Cork line. I was originally from Castletown near
Portlaoise. I came into the permanent way on the 31st July 1952. I came in
under inspector John Wilson in Portlaoise and I worked for three months on a
resleepering job. When that was finished, I moved off to Athy. This was for the
season when there was beet traffic. I worked on the Ballylinan branch which was
only opened for the beet season. It was in very poor condition, it was just keeping it right, putting in sleepers. So I worked on that for three months and then
joined up with John Downey doing yard relaying. We travelled a good bit, we
were around Mageney, Bagnalstown, Clonmel, Rosslare Strand and other places.

I worked on the Matisa tamper. It was very small, just like a wagon. You had
to work it manually. I was on that for two or three years. It was the high technology of those days. Sometimes the work wouldn't be too good because the ballast
formation wasn't great. If you had a hard bed you had a job to pack it. You had
to double pack the joints. It didn't line the track, it was levelled by the men in
front of you and you just packed the sleepers. I travelled all over the whole system. I wasn't that keen on it. There wasn't work enough in it for me. You could
be stuck in sidings and I wouldn't be happy if there wasn't manual working.

Some people liked it but I didn't think I was made for it. After a few years I went back to my gang again. Eventually Jack Healy, the chief inspector in Waterford came out and asked me if I would be interested in another job, so I said: 'It all depends.' He put me on lifting and lining with a telescopic arrangement that you clamp on the rail and you were sighting it as they jacked the track. I was at that for a while. The Waterford Area was being changed, now they weren't doing the Cork line. So there was a bit of a problem then for the chief inspector; he was based in Waterford. He asked me would I transfer to his area. So I said: 'I probably will but I'd have to go in digs, then I would have no money left.' So eventually he came up to me and said: I'll give you a ganger's job in Clonmel yard and with a bit more money.' I was only a platelayer at that time. I took it up anyway. I was appointed a ganger in Clonmel and I never worked in it. He took me off and we started doing points and crossings. And I was at that and relaying for a few years. In 1963 I was appointed inspector in Enniscorthy. In 1969 they closed down that inspector's division and I was transferred to Waterford, and I was an inspector there until 1974.

The line to Dungarvan was open then for the dolomite ore traffic. The line was in pretty good condition. I finished off the Ballinacourty turnout and sidings. When we took the land for the connection up to Ballinacourty, it was nearly three miles and we were building the railway. They were market garden farmers there and we took the good land and one farmer wasn't too pleased. We had to put in level crossings. In one place early one morning we were putting in a gate and the farmer came along and took me aside and said: 'You are not putting up any gates here.' I said: 'I don't know, but I have an order to put them up anyway.' He said: 'If you continue to put them up, I have a gun inside and I'll shoot you.' I said: 'Go ahead but I'm going to put up the gates anyway. Whether you'll shoot me or not, someone will have to bury me and you'll wind up without seeing anyone for a long time.' So anyway, he went off in and he came out in about a half an hour in his car. He drove out and he nearly tore down the gates. We put them up and we never heard any more from then. I was in Waterford for a while when we took up the line that was going to Dungarvan. All of that track was recycled. I then went back to Wexford in 1974 and was there until 1979. The Dublin Division took over Waterford around 1977. David Waters came, he was then divisional engineer in Dublin and asked me would I come to the Dublin Suburban project, building what was afterwards called the DART. He was to head it up. I considered it and eventually I decided: 'yes.' I went to Dublin then from 1979 until the finish of it and I came back to Wexford at the end. I was there for a few months and I headed off down to Ballybrophy. It was a big job and it lasted only four months and worked on the Dublin-Cork line around Sallins. I then went back to Wexford.

Eventually Mr. O' Donoghue came down and asked would I go to Portlaoise Rail Depot. I went and I was there for ten years. It was completely different. You didn't have time to think. You had more staff and you were more confined. It was more of a factory situation than out on the track. The big push for relaying was only coming. We increased the sleepers from 236 per day for one shift, to over 840 in two shifts. Apart from the sleepers everything else increased as well; you had more track panels going out and coming in. The Donelli gangs were increased from one to two and then to three. The welding gangs eventually went from one to four. The big problem was it was difficult to get possessions. There was more time lost getting in and getting out. On a Sunday you'd be lucky to get a quarter of a mile done. Then we got block relaying; you'd get the track for five or six weeks and got a new rail train to bring out the CWR; everything was improved. I finished up eventually in the depot on 28 Oct 1998 when I was aged 65 years. When I retired I went back to Portlaoise for a year. I relaid all the sidings, 19 turnouts in the yard. I came back to Dublin to work. I got an offer of another job in Waterford, a heritage railway. It was from Kilmeaden to Waterford; it didn't cross the river. It went down to the old station, the first for the Mallow to Waterford. It was down by the foundry, all overgrown. Initially they planned to go just where the bridge was but I said you could go down this way. It was all overgrown, trees and bushes. We cleared it all anyway. I gave six and a half years at it full-time. They are doing well, it's a tourist attraction.

I'll tell you a few good things which happened in my time. We were going around with John Downey and we had the old-type sleeping vans at the station. You had to pay one and sixpence a night for your bunk. There was a section where you could cook, an old oven, a cooker running on coal or timber. There were 12 of us in it. We went to Thurles one day and we were staying that night and the van was there. We had to stay in the van. There were two compartments, six bunks each, three on top of one another. There were no sheets or blankets there, even though they were supposed to be supplied. It was winter time and we had to use newspapers and oil skins. A fellow got in on the top bunk and he called out: 'What kind of blankets and sheets do you have, I have the Irish Independent under me?' That was Mick Keane, he was an inspector in Carlow afterwards.

They were doing relaying between Mountrath and Portlaoise. There was no such thing as possessions, you had your timetable and you put out your flagmen in between trains. You worked between. Two flagmen out each side and you might get two lengths in each time. They were doing this mile of resleepering on a Sunday. The parish priest of Mountrath came out and asked the ganger: 'What are you doing here?' 'We're resleepering this section of track. It's gone bad, we have to renew it.' And the priest said: 'Will it be a good job?' The ganger said: 'It will.' The priest said: 'I don't think it will be a good job. You know you are breaking the Sabbath.' A lot more things passed. He asked who was the head man. He said that he would write to them; I don't know if he did or not, but he was very annoyed.

We didn't do scarcely any Sunday work. When I was temporary we only got one Sunday in the year. The weekend work came in around the late 60s. In the old days also you never got expenses. We had to pay our digs out of our own money. I remember in 1952 or 1954 we were getting less than four pounds a week. The digs would be 50 shillings. Then you had to pay your tax out of it. You got breakfast, dinner and tea in the digs but you were lucky if you had a

Right. Plan of a section of the D & KR, showing the line crossing the Grand Canal and the Dodder. (Iarnród Éireann)

Clockwise from below: the Portstewart Tramway being lifted after closure in 1926; share certificate for the Newry & Armagh Railway Company; at work on a narrow-gauge line in Antrim; ceremonial mahogany wheelbarrow from the opening of the Enniskillen, Bundoran & Sligo Railway in 1866. (Ulster Folk & Transport Museum)

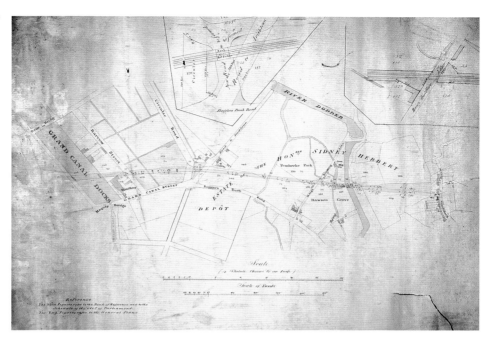

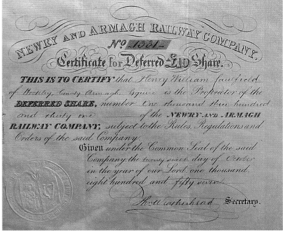

pound left. I remember being in Bagnalstown relaying plain track and turnouts and being in Mageney. It was a very wet day. We had a ballast train and wagons. We had to put out all the ballast and the sleepers. The morning became bad and you wouldn't put out a duck, it was so awful. There were about 30 of us and we had to work that day in the rain, all day. It was typical: we weren't supplied with anything – boots, coats or anything. The rain was so bad that we took off all our clothes, bar our pants. It was wintertime but you'd be hacking and sweating, you'd be warm enough. We worked all day and we had to cycle back eight miles to our digs that evening. We worked from eight to half five. We went back and we had to put an old coat over us it was so wet. We had our dinner in the digs that evening. Then we went back down to the station in Athy that night and we lit a fire in the old hut and dried our clothes for the next morning.

We were all young, in our twenties. It was all hard work, you worked through. You got your lunch at one o'clock and you got nothing until you went home in the evening. Years ago there was no such thing as a ten o'clock break. Fellows would be trying to get a sup of tea at nine o'clock, maybe outside in the ditch, but eventually it came in. We had no vans then, you had to get to site on bicycles. You went directly to where the work was. Any rails or sleepers were brought out by ballast train. That's the way it worked. The rain didn't matter, you continued working. You just got your head down in the morning. The ganger, the man in charge, he never worked. He'd walk up and down all day. He'd walk on the sleepers, maybe with a whistle to warn of a train coming, and he'd be swinging it in his hand, and every move you made, he'd be walking behind you. They worked the men hard. You wouldn't lift your head. Funny enough, we enjoyed it. You had to load rails by hand then, 45 foot rails. There would be 25 men to a rail length. We were throwing them by hand up from the side of the track. You'd be stretched out, throwing them onto a wagon. You'd load a mile of rails on a Sunday. Lifting sleepers, there would be two men to a sleeper. But when it had chairs on it there would be two men in front with a beater handle holding it and one lad carrying it behind.

One time we did a mile and a quarter of resleepering down between Thurles and Templemore on a Sunday. Martin Culliton was the chief inspector in Waterford. Men were brought in for this. Everyone had to get there under their own steam. I had to get up in the morning and cycle 22 miles. We arrived in Templemore and went to seven o'clock Mass there. We started work then and we got one break, at lunchtime. The job was running on till ten o'clock that Sunday night. Someone went to light a fire for a cup of tea and the chief inspector came up and put the fire out and we got nothing. We finished at ten that night and I had to cycle 22 miles home after that. It was near morning by the time I got home, although I felt alright. I was fit then, I used to hurl and did cross-country running.

Tools like bars were left out at night by the side, where we were working. On a frosty morning in winter time we had to heat the bars on a fire. Otherwise the bars would stick to your hand as we had no gloves then. Also, the tea in the billy can would sometimes freeze in the can before we'd have it drunk.

Another time, at the end of 1954, I was working down between Ballybrophy and Lisduff. The inspection car was coming from Waterford with Mr. Meleady and Jack Healy, the chief inspector. You always got word that they were coming. I remember it well it was five past eight in the winter. There was frost there, even on the bushes. The ganger said we'll take off our coats now and we were in our shirt and pants digging away. In the winter frost, there we were. The car came by and I don't know what they thought of us, in our shirts, with the sweat coming out of us. They must have thought we were mad. That's the way people worked, gangers and all. They were terrified of engineers or boss-men. In those days you would have to salute the district engineer. They would only talk about business, nothing else. They'd check you on everything. The Chief Engineer Mr. Large, was like God in my time. If he asked you a question and you didn't answer right he was very strict. He'd go through in the inspection car and stop at all the gangs. He'd ask you some questions, what you were doing, what you should and shouldn't be doing. If there was something wrong, he'd let you know fairly quick. The inspectors were afraid of him. Everyone worked that time in fear. It was military style. You didn't hang around and discipline was very tight. You did what you were told and, if you didn't, you were told out you go. I've seen people told to go home and go about their business. You had no comeback. You were blackened for all time. It was a hard grind. It amuses me to see how it's become for people today. It's good for them but it's gone from one extreme to the other. I think it's gone too far now. You tell people to do things now and they have every excuse, they have all sorts of reasons why they can't do this.

Back to the inspector's time: he was in charge of his division. His job was to walk part every day, some days he'd walk seven or eight miles. He might walk three or four days in a week. You had to walk as well as the men. On some days I walked 20 mile of track. You checked it all, gauged it, noted it. On another day you did the timesheets and then another day you'd be doing stock. Sometimes you'd have to go out at eight o'clock to organise the gangs. There were no vans or company cars. You'd have to walk or cycle or maybe go by train. You had the rail bikes then. The inspector had them, they were on them the whole time. They'd know when the train was coming. When they saw one, they'd get off and lift off the bike. Going around sharp curves you'd have to be very careful. The inspector had only a single rail bike, but there was a double when the chief inspector was brought.

When I started off there were no Sundays. No overtime, just the bare basic pay. Later, during the time of the DART I got no time off. Quite often in that time, I worked hard but I never stayed in Dublin, My wife said I was mad. My sons didn't see me for a good few years. I had neighbours and they never saw me – they often wondered was I around at all. The weekend was when we could work away all the time. We were understaffed then. There were so many jobs on. When I was working the suburban, we often had eight ballast trains coming out of North Wall to do a job for different places. They were all loaded with stuff and they had to be organised. At that time I had thirty lookout men alone, apart from other staff. No matter where they were working they had to come to

LMS THE PERMANENT WAY
RELAYING

by Stanhope Forbes R.A.

Above. 'The Permanent Way', a poster commissioned by the London Midland & Scottish Railway in 1922. (Science and Society Picture Library)

Left. All together: permanent way men lift a rail while restoring the track after a derailment at Hybla, south of Monasterevan, on the Dublin-Cork line in 1959. (National Library of Ireland)

Above. Many men, all working by hand. At a junction at Portadown, around the early part of the mid 20th century. The man with the hat, centre right, is most likely the Permanent Way Inspector. (Ulster Folk & Transport Museum)

Right. On assignment with Mozambique railways in the early 1990s: Chief Inspector Denis Redmond, second from left, Inspector John Ryan, fourth from left. (CIÉ)

Connolly and sign in at seven in the morning and sign off there in the evening, to make sure they were there, because it happened a couple of times, people supposed to be there and they never showed up. I suppose yes, I'd look back on the DART time as my finest hour. I have to say I had great workers. They were from every county in Ireland. And I had Dublin people on it and they were right good people. And a lot of them got good jobs out of it. Some are inspectors. I'd say there's no bad worker, there are no bad people. Another thing I'd say: a man is only as good as his master. If you show people what to do, and look after them and tell them if they are doing wrong, they will always come around.

In the DART times, I came up to Dublin in December 1979, and I was walking around here for two months, sizing up the thing. I had no men, no tools – nothing. I was kind of getting fed up. Eventually I got three regular fellows. I shifted around and I gathered a few men and I got going. I'd say that eventually, on the DART alone, I put around a thousand people through my hands. There were times when I had about three or four hundred fellows working for me. They were nearly all raw, I took them in from all walks of life. They all worked out very well. I was only a small cog in the machine, but with regard to track-work, we finished on time, we finished on budget.

In the old days, the people who did the relaying were only temporary men. There were no vans and you'd have to get to jobs on your own. You'd meet up with others at crossroads. If they weren't there at the time, you'd go ahead. You'd get a wisp of grass from the ditch and fling it on the road, so when the other fellow came up he'd know that you had gone on, he wouldn't be waiting for you.

At that time every man had his own little billycan. You lit a fire and you poured in the tea and sugar. You could have about 30 cans on the fire. The fire would be made up of sleepers and it would be blazing up around the can, no lid on it. And you put a matchstick into the can to keep the smoke from going into the tea. You'd break off a matchstick, not put in the red part, and that would keep the smoke from the tea. Then if you had a rasher or egg you'd clean the shovel, take the butter off the bread and fry it on the shovel over the fire. It was very tasty. People were starving with the hunger then. You used to get your breakfast at six o'clock in the morning. It was one o'clock that day before you were allowed put your mouth to anything. You'd be working from eight o'clock and working hard. You'd be looking up to see the ganger with a whistle, and he wouldn't call it until a minute to one o' clock. A man would have been given an hour to light the fire. On a wet day he'd have a problem lighting it and if he didn't there would be murder then. The fellow who lit the fire: he'd always have his own can boiled and that of the gangers. It didn't matter after that. You had 45 minutes for your break. You'd be mad hungry, you'd have sandwiches and have rashers the odd time. It was sort of a treat. You'd nearly eat a loaf of bread you'd be so hungry.

People don't realise now how things have changed for the better. We were lucky to get the investment in the railway in recent years. Just in the last year money has come to be tight all across the country. However, the railway has a future and I think the wheel will turn again.

Michael Keane
Permanent Way Inspector, Carlow, retired.

I was only 18 years of age when I joined in 1949. I'm from near Cashel. My brother was already working on the railway. I started down at Limerick Junction, with Jimmy Moore the permanent way inspector. They were relaying down there. That time we had to relay with it all done by hack and shovel. No machinery. You had a half length, eight boxes we used to call it. There were 15 boxes in the length, a 45 foot rail. There would be two of us in the length and we'd have to clean out the boxes and there would be two ahead of us and two behind. We had to shovel it up the bank. I remember one day in Carlow, a wagon load of ashes came to Bagnalstown, this was in the steam days. You'd have to shovel it out down the bank. We were out on a Sunday morning out of Bagnalstown; the line is way up beyond the fields. There was a terrible wind blowing. There were a lot of us up on the wagon and you'd throw out a shovel load and half of it would come back on top of you with the wind. When we had it all done we were so black you could hardly see. We went back into Bagnalstown and we had to go to the north side of the station and take up old sleepers. The Inspector wouldn't give us time to clean ourselves. 'Come on, get up on the train, you can clean yourselves when you get home.'

And then I worked in the Junction. My grandfather worked on the railway for years, on the Cashel branch, which is closed for years. He got me a job with the loco in Thurles. The day I got word, I was still on the job with Jimmy Moore in the Junction, so I didn't go to the loco at all, I stayed with the permanent way. Later we were paid off in Limerick Junction. We were coming home, myself and a man called Jack McCarthy. We were coming home and we saw the ESB lads down in the field. We didn't know if we'd get back on the railway so we decided to go down and ask whoever was the foreman was there any chance of a job. They were digging holes for the poles. 'You can start in the morning. You have to dig three holes a day', he says. 'If they're hard, I'll give you a hand, I'll get you another man'. Jasus, I had the three holes dug by two o'clock. The foreman said: 'It doesn't matter what time you have them dug at, that's all you do'. We got on great, we started on a Friday. I went in Saturday morning and when I came home, in the afternoon, it was a half day; there was word for me there was work in the permanent way in Thurles. So I sent word Monday morning to the foreman of the ESB that I wasn't going in. I had to collect my wages, so I went over. I got 17 shillings for the day and a half and I've been on the railway ever since. I chose to go back, my grandfather was on it, and my brother was on it.

We worked in Goold's Cross, all the way up the line, whatever had to be done, relaying. We used to do the crossings in the yards. We did Ballybrophy; it was Chief Inspector Mahony in Waterford. He had a son who was an inspector afterwards. There's a Limerick line in Ballybrophy as well, it's the junction for Limerick. So there were nine crossings built for that crossover, it was a bag of tricks, we called it. It was complicated; there were so many crossings and switches. I was at that for ages. John Downey was the ganger that time. He had a caravan in the station. One half was for eating and sleeping and the other half was for the tools. We worked in the yard at Mageney. One wet Saturday we were loading the wagons with shovels. And the rain came down in tons after dinner. Myself and another man, we took off our shirts, we were so wet we worked with only the trousers on us. When the job had started, hail rain or snow, you had to finish the job.

With no machinery it was tough in the early days. Later on we had JCB's and the Priestman crane for loading. I had good days and bad days, more good than bad. Most of our problems were gauge. The relaying was very hard before the machines came out. Relaying through banks, you'd have to take out the sleeper with two chairs on it and you'd be trying to get it up the bank with four men. As well we'd be loading rails by hand. You'd have to lift them up and put them up on a wagon. Everything was hard; it was all done by shovel or hand. We had to load the sleepers by hand when we were bringing them on the sleeper train into the station for stocktaking. Sometimes the ballast would be low, the wagon high or on a curve. It would be very difficult. Then later on, we used to pile ten sleepers with the Priestman, put a chain under them and lift them up, that was a great advantage.

I retired in 1994. I had a bypass before that and I haven't looked back since. I enjoyed my time on the railway. I had run-ins with the lads, up and down, but I never sacked anybody. I'll be 80 on the 9th of April 2009. I miss the railway. If I was talking to a railway man, that's all we'd be talking about, the railway. You never forget it.

Vincent Moran
Patrol Ganger, Manulla, retired.

I worked for CIÉ and it was all cycling, you had to cycle hither and thither everywhere at that time. I was often on with the ESB in 1954 when the electrification was around here. We got three pounds ten shillings and a penny with the ESB. I joined CIÉ and we started refettling from Balla to Westport. We did all that for four pounds ten shillings and a penny. A pound extra. The ten pound bag of flour was around ten shillings at the time. John Mc Donnell, he was an inspector at Claremorris, he used to cycle up along there. I remember one man who used to cycle from Manulla to Tuam. That's a fierce spin from Manulla. It's at least 30 miles.

After that you had the ordinary maintenance and you were left off that for a while. I was temporary at that time. It was very hard to get permanent. I got permanent later on, but I had to leave after my brother got sick, Lord have mercy on him. The job in general was alright, but there was nothing soft in it in my time. You went out there in the morning and you had no ten o'clock break and it was all belt out bolts, there was no gas, nothing. The bolts would be flying through the bushes. It was dangerous. We had to lift up the rails by hand onto the wagons. I'll tell you, the work rotated, you could be on for three months or for six months. I was taken on permanent in the 60s.

I worked for Jimmy Loughnane, the inspector. There wasn't a man from Ballina to Inchicore that didn't know him. He was a type of individual, he was very strict. He was fair in some ways. He asked me: 'What do you, Vincey, think of me?' I said: 'I'll tell you now, you're your own worst enemy.' And he said: 'How do you make out that?' I replied: 'You're running in and out to hospital with high blood pressure, over what? Many a man came here and you'll be gone and so will I.' Paddy Hunt came down to build crossovers and John Cronin the chief inspector would come down to check it out.

I always regretted the weekend work. In order to make a week's wages you had to do it. My wife and children weren't happy about it, they still tell me this today. I remember one inspector saying: 'I require as many men as possible, working at such and such on a Sunday.' You were expected to do it. I retired in the 80s. The relaying that I saw after was a big change from the way we were.

Liam Brennan
Permanent Way Inspector, Wexford, retired.

I started in a relaying gang in 1955 up around Wellington Bridge. I remember at that time, we were pressing rails. They were flat-bottom, you had to curve the rail. I remember the weather was brutal – it was around January – snow, frost and ice. When you were temporary, you had no protective clothing. There were about twenty in a gang, a lot of them had come over the ditch, fellows with no experience, like myself. You got laid off that time fairly constant, as there was a big recession, all through that era, in the 40s and 50s, the money was scarce. People were very glad of the work. It was one of the better jobs at the time. Mostly lads were working with farmers. You travelled long journeys. You had to stop in digs. If you got Saturday overtime you were delighted, you could pay for the digs.

My grandfather worked on the making of the Waterford-Rosslare line. McAlpine were the contractors. My grandfather told me about the fellows that worked on the building of the line. One man, his name was Walsh, he walked from the Forth mountain, just up here, to the work; it was 12 or 14 miles to where they were building the railway, around Duncormick. He'd bring a bit of bread in his pack. When he got there in the morning, he'd sit down and eat the bit of bread. They used to start work at half seven. He'd work all day then, to half five or six o'clock. He'd had a bit of bread at midday. He'd walk back at the end of the day. It was pretty tough. His mother was a semi-invalid and he had to go home to mind her. He worked on the railway as long as he could and then the works moved on and he had to give it up. There was a lot of work here at Rosslare, with the works on the pier. It was said that if you weren't in your shirt-sleeves that McAlpine didn't keep you. In cold weather, some of the lads used to put the shirt over the jumper. I heard my grandfather tell another story about a cutting where they had to cut to lower the ground. After that there was a valley. There's a bridge in Duncormick that's similar to the Taylorstown Viaduct, it's only a three-span. There was a long approach that they had to fill up and they drew that from the cutting with horses. They backed in the horse to tip up the earth, over a steep drop. There were certain times when they went back too far and the cart would break away from the horse and tip down. There was one particular time when the cart and horse went down. The horse was killed. They left them all there. They threw the fill down on top of them.

I was made permanent on the railway in 1968. I was ganger on the static gang here at Rosslare Strand. Then I started doing relief inspector in Waterford and Wicklow. Dan Donovan then went to do the DART in 1979 and I took over as acting inspector. I got the full-time inspector's job around 1987.

We had lots of derailments during the beet season with wagons. You'd get a call every night that wagons were off the road. They'd only be hopping off at hand points. I enjoyed it all. I missed it for a long time when I retired. It was getting interesting. The new rail had come in about four years before I retired. In the old days you'd be out on a Sunday relaying by hand. You could go out on the morning and it would be bucketing down rain and you'd be struggling, and you'd look back in the evening and you'd only have done half of what you planned. Fellows were tired and weary and wet and cold. Now with the Donellis the train would come down and by three thirty you'd have put in half a mile. It was an unbelievable change. I did some of the big programme of relaying with the CWR in Wicklow. Lord almighty, that was a great change. And some of that Wicklow division was brutal. It was nobody's fault but it was run into the ground. There was nobody could do anything with it. You were out repairing something that shouldn't have been in the road. I remember I went up to relieve the inspector, Mick Smullen, who was going on holidays. I remember the second day I was there, there were broken rails reported. I said: 'I wonder will I go back to Wexford?' Things have changed for the better.

There was a kind of weeding out process in the old days. Fellows would be taken on and they couldn't stick it. The ones who stayed on got attached to it. There was a ban on appointment in the 1950s and 1960s. They were taking on temporary men, then they'd lay you off after a year and nine months; that way they didn't have to appoint you.

There was another instance up in Ballycullane. There was an inspector, he was a very cross man. There was a rail van, with all the tools. It was pushed into a siding. They were trying to get a rail in, they were pressing a rail. He said: 'Go down to the van and get the press.' There was an old timer down making the tea and the fellow said: 'I want the press.' He handed him the newspaper, the *Irish Press*. He brought it up to the inspector and I wouldn't tell you what the inspector said to him.

My two sons are driving trains now, they stayed in the railway. One is in Sligo. The other drives the Rosslare train. I also have a grandson who is a train driver in Connolly Station.

Neilus O' Donoghue
Assistant Chief Civil Engineer, retired.

I started in British Rail in 1956. We were doing the upgrade of what is now called the West Coast Main Line. A group of us more or less came back together in 1959. At that time Dan Herlihy was the overall Chief Engineer. Somerville Large was his deputy dealing with the civils. Large, at my first interview, said: 'Where are you from?' I said: 'I'm from West Cork.' 'I'm a West Cork man too', he said. He came from Castle Townsend. A lot of engineers were appointed at that time, around ten. I was selected and went to Cork.

The permanent way work at that time was almost completely manual. The Chief Engineer was keen to introduce mechanisation. As a junior engineer I was quickly introduced to weekend working to do work study on the methods then in use, so that improvements could be made.

I moved to Limerick in 1960. The next big thing was the setting up of the area management structure in 1961. When I joined, there were four district engineers: Waterford, Cork, Dublin and Limerick. Then that was changed to five areas; Galway was added. Gerry Cleary, who was assistant in Cork, went to Galway and set up the office there.

Things were very tight, and they managed to keep the thing going. Because, as Large said: 'The British didn't leave us much, but they left us the railway.' He was very strict, but he was very good. He did bark, but it was all an act to keep you going. He would treat you with a view that your career would move. Large taught us about the railway. Pat Jennings brought Large back and showed him the DART when it was opened. He was very old at this time but he was amazed and delighted at the progress that was made.

Arthur Plumer was the district engineer in Westland Row. He was downstairs and Large was upstairs. When Large went on holidays, he was acting chief. Everything he wanted to try and get done, he'd write up to Large. Then he'd go upstairs and answer that and give out holy hell to himself.

There was a story about himself and Bob Stevens, who was a junior engineer then. Plumer was keen to develop accuracy of the highest calibre in him. He instructed him: 'Stevens, I want you to go out to Dalkey. There's a stone wall there that a neighbour is complaining about. I want you to survey that wall. Bring it in to me and make sure that you do it right this time.' Bob went out. He even got the ganger to expose the foundation. He got every stone set out, height, width and everything. He noted the ivy on it. He presented the drawing and Plumer said: 'Very good, very good, you seem to be coming on. What was the mortar made of, Stevens?' 'Don't know, Mr. Plumer.' 'Next time I send you on a survey, you should do it properly.' Plumer was a very good engineer.

T.S. Harman in Cork was a pure gentleman. His salary didn't pay his income tax. Why he came to work I don't know. Most of the land round the railway was from his forebears. His biggest expression was: 'By Jove, you don't tell me so.' He was a very gentlemanly type. John Hyde Ffolliott was very austere and kept his distance. When the area engineer system came in Harman, Hyde Ffolliott and, I think, Plumer retired then. The area system under area management worked until 1980. It didn't work as each of these five areas could not afford to have machines of their own. There was a need to invest in the infrastructure. It was then decided to have three divisions: Dublin, Limerick Junction and Athlone. Waterford and Galway were closed.

After Limerick I was on projects working for D.J. O' Connor who was new works engineer. He told me this story: 'In 1922 I was preparing to go to Trinity College and was studying Latin in Cork. One evening after leaving Mallow station I walked home which was some distance away. Sometime later there were several large explosions which demolished the arched Mallow Viaduct over which the train I had just used had passed. Later that night, a lorry rushed into our place, several Irregulars jumped out, demanding lodgings for the night. Amongst these were Dev and Liam Lynch My father, who was Cork County Engineer, gave out to them: "Ragamuffins blowing up bridges, and I will have to rebuild them." I had to give up my bed to Dev as I was over six feet. We were peeping through the kitchen door to see what bombs Dev carried in his haversack but we were disappointed when he only pulled out dry socks.'

I was appointed as assistant area engineer in Waterford in 1966. I went to Athlone in 1975. Every bit of the MGWR was flat bottom rail. The only thing that was wrong with it were the fastenings – they only had a spike. The weight of the rail in 1896 in the Midland was greater than in Germany; German railways had only around a 90 lb rail then, the Midland had 95 lb. This was very heavy rail for a rail network that only carried cattle and very few people.

I was in Athlone until 1980, then I moved to Dublin when Pat Jennings was made chief, working as his assistant chief. I retired in 1995.

Pat Jennings
Chief Civil Engineer, retired.

I joined the railway in 1960. I worked on the tunnelling in England from the end of 1951 till 1956. At that time I started off with the tunnelling contractors, Waddingtons. I was an engineer in London, building near King's Cross. You had to build a tunnel around other tunnels. To get to the other side you had to crawl on your stomach and go through dirt and dust and clay to get to do surveying or whatever. After a few years I got notification that I'd have to do National Service. I was married at this time. There was a job coming up in North Wales. I went up there, it was putting in thousands of piles for a power station. That job was finishing up when, one day, two gentlemen, who looked military, came in. We talked and then they said: 'You know, Mr. Jennings, you have to do the National Service.' I replied that I wouldn't have any interest in doing it. They came back a month later and laid it on the line: 'If you don't report to such and such Barracks by the first of August you have to be gone out of the country.' So I came back to Ireland and worked for contractors here.

I applied for a job in the railway around 1959. The reason was I used to charge for my car to go from my digs to the site and they wouldn't allow that. That cheesed me off. I got the job in the railway. Paddy Somerville Large was the Chief Civil Engineer. Dan Herlihy was the overall Chief Engineer in charge

Above. Eyes down, two men pedal the rail bicycle on the single track along the coast, of the Belfast-Larne line, near Whitehead. Is that the Chief Permanent Way Inspector in the middle? (Ulster Folk & Transport Museum)

Right. Renewal of Underbridge 65 (Quagmire Bridge) on the Tralee branch in 1956. (Iarnród Éireann)

of both civil and mechanical. Somerville Large was very pleasant. He was really a gentleman. But he suffered fools badly. There was no such thing as foolish talk for him. You had to give him straight answers. If you did, and you didn't show any fear of him, there was no problem. Many people were afraid of him because he'd cut the ground from under you. Not so much a sarcastic remark, but you'd tell him something and he'd say: 'Yes, is that so now?' That'd be the end of it.

Then I worked on the oil tank installation and big retaining walls in Inchicore. I became new works engineer around 1965. Michael Gill joined CIÉ earlier, maybe 1963. His project was the demolishing of all of Broadstone; he took up the track and converted it. Dan Herlihy used to walk the ground with Michael who was able to do estimates very quickly. Dan would do estimates item by item, but Michael would do a broad estimate. Dan thought highly of him. Dan at that time had moved up to Assistant General Manager.

Large retired because his wife was not well. We used to go out to his house near Fassaroe in Bray. Valimbrosa was the name. There was a big long avenue into it. He used to privately produce apples, with a huge orchard and sell these. We used to be invited out to avail of the windblown apples. He'd entertain us, his wife would bring us in and give us sandwiches. He was very nice that way.

Michael Gill was appointed Chief Civil Engineer. The first task Dan gave him was to install the first CWR and get that going. Then he went on to be General Manager of the Great Southern Hotels. Dan Herlihy regretted losing his young protégé from the civil engineers.

When he left I acted as Chief Civil Engineer for six months. I moved into the office took over the role and confounded everyone. I enjoyed it, it was great crack. I called divisional engineer's meetings and chaired these. About six months later Crawford Yates was appointed. He was divisional engineer at the time. I got £500 for my efforts. It was a big lot at the time and at least it was a token. I then went on to replace Yates in the Dublin Division. It was different and I didn't know anything about that kind of work. But I had the best guy that would bring you on, Denis Redmond. He took the time to go out and explain all to me. Every single thing, he explained as we went along. After six months, I was fairly conversant. I must have been five years as divisional engineer, that was the time they were doing the resignalling as well. Then the remanning and mechanisation came. So I went back to Pearse as assistant chief civil engineer for maintenance of way. I did all the schemes for the mechanisation and the remanning. I travelled around the country dealing with all the redundancies and the voluntary severance and reduced the numbers of men considerably. David Waters had replaced me in the division. Then I was appointed Chief Civil Engineer in 1980. The Dublin Suburban project had started. David Waters had moved from the division around the end of 1979 to prepare the DART programme. Crawford Yates retired two years early due to health problems. One day, Anne Morris, the general manager's secretary, rang me up and said: 'The General Manager wants to see you.' I said: 'What did he want to see me about?' 'Come up', she said, 'It will be worth your while'. So, I went up and the General Manager, Jack Higgins, gave me the job. I hadn't any real bother with the chief civil engineer's job. I was just busy. I had been doing the maintenance of way job for four or five years. So I knew the whole system. I thought I was reasonably capable for the job. I enjoyed it. Jack Higgins was a big support.

I was also in charge of the canals. I had done it with the new works job, after that it became a full time job for Brendan Daly and, after that, Pat Hannigan. There used to be a million pounds to spend and that's all. When I was Chief Engineer one of my duties was canal inspection. I used to spend two or three days at that. One of the trips was to hire a boat and go down the Barrow as far as St. Mullins and back up again. I generally took Molly, my wife, and Conor, my grandson, on this trip.

I retired in 1995. Earlier in 1993 I did a stint in Albanian Railways (this was through CIÉ Consult). We arrived in Durres where the railway headquarters was. The first day we had to go to the southern end of the railway by train and we had to bring our swimming togs. The whole office nearly came on the trip. We came back in one of the big jeeps. I remember the windscreen was all broken. In Albania no-one ever replaced a windscreen. The stay there was a pleasant experience.

Another consultancy assignment was when I went to Uganda around 1989. We were arrested in Uganda. The whole team. We were sitting in the office in Kampala for two or three weeks before we ever saw a bit of track. I was going stone mad to get out. We persuaded the project manager that there was an inspection car up in the yard and to get it set up. So I went up one day, whatever shunting they had done, the inspection car was down at the end of a row of sidings. There were two or three trains in front of it. We had started down there at nine o'clock. By pressurising and God knows what, we eventually got the car out. We set off and the car was loaded with plenty of hangers on. People for opening gates, with lots of people hanging around. We went off anyway and we must have travelled one or two hundred miles along at a fair clip. We came to the Owens Falls dam. The track ran alongside one of the reservoirs. So we stopped to take some photographs. Then, next thing, out of the underbrush this band of military appeared and came up to us and challenged us. We hadn't a permit to take photographs and we were arrested. We weren't allowed back into the inspection car. They had an open lorry somewhere nearby. We were taken down this embankment, away from the Owens Falls. We pleaded with them, we said that you can take the camera and the film. It was no good. Some of the people in the inspection car, including the project manager, hadn't got out and they weren't arrested. They were told to go about their business. Myself, Dick Grainger (then Chief Mechanical Engineer) and an economist were arrested. We were carted around in the back of the truck. The soldiers were only boys. I was sitting beside one of these fellows. They had these guns with the holes in the barrels. They were all armed to the teeth. I tried to engage them in conversation, but it wasn't any good, as most couldn't speak English. They brought us to a town and through this up to their barracks. At around the same time the project manager must have gotten a message to Kampala and orders came down that we were to be let go. We were taken back into the centre of the town and let off in the street. Someone eventually came down from the station and picked us up.

There was a story told about Dan Herlihy. This was somewhere up around Cabra. They were doing some big layout at the cattle yard up there. Dan arrived on the job and he was walking around. He called over the inspector. He said: 'What in the name of God are those men doing up there? They are doing nothing standing up there. Sack them immediately!' The poor inspector was looking around, to see what excuse he could give. He thought it was his own men when all of a sudden it dawned on him that: 'They're not my men, they belong to the Posts and Telegraphs.'

They started the concrete sleepers just after the war. The quality of the native timber was hopeless. They tried larch. You could put out larch and in maybe six months time there would be a lot of fungus growing on it. The quality of sleepers was a struggle. That was when plan patching came in, you'd only put in a new sleeper when everything was exhausted. You'd take the existing sleepers and shove them on a bit, you'd have a new base to work with and redrill.

They kept going with the concrete. People started going abroad to inspect developments there. We were one of the first railways to go all diesel in Europe, but that was because we couldn't get the coal either. The concrete sleeper plant was producing the initial sleepers. They worked quite well but they were heavy to handle. Somebody went to Germany and got in touch with Dywidag and got better moulds, which were used for manufacture in the Concrete Bank at Inchicore. Unfortunately we penny-pinched and we started off with a poorer model of sleeper, cheaper than that of the Germans who had a higher axle loading. The dieselisation had come in, the axle loads were quite heavy. They didn't have the big wheel of the steam engines to spread the load. The diesels were impacting more significantly on this cheap sleeper. It was splitting and breaking. They made lots of mistakes. They didn't put in pads. It cut down into the concrete. Then they put in timber pads. They were of poor quality and squeezed out. Eventually we did get a high quality pad.

When Michael Gill was appointed as Chief Civil Engineer, as I mentioned, his first task was the introduction of CWR. That was when the 'Golden Mile' was put in. From that time, the quality of the concrete sleeper improved a lot. It was still made here in Inchicore. Then Michael introduced the 50 kg rail. There was a theory that each chief engineer should have his own rail. I know Large fiddled around and modified a number of rails. The MGWR designed their own rails, there was no equivalent rail in another railway. They'd produce a profile every time a railway was modified or changed.

The Golden Mile went on for a long time. It was 87 lb bullhead rail, with keys, welded by the aluminothermic method. However, everything had to be done on the cheap with the result that, on the Golden Mile, in later years most of the welds failed from fatigue. We did use ultrasonic testing then. We always identified risky welds, cutting them out and restressing. The 87 lb was fine except that the key was never a satisfactory restraint.

When the 50 kg came in everyone thought we were on the pig's back, because we had a good big flat-bottomed rail. I remember John Cronin, the then chief inspector in Athlone, saying that when the first 50 kg rail went across the Shannon it was a big occasion because, up to then, the only rails they had got were second-hand. This must have been since the 1900s as the bulk of the rails, the 95 lbs, were bought at the turn of the century. These were from 1898 to around 1905 on the MGWR. This was all in the west, the only bit of the MGWR here was from Mullingar up to Dublin. As a result of these old rails, there had been different kinds of defects. Some of them had to be taken out straight away when detected. Others had to be walked daily. Every possible fracture or failure would occur with them. They were old and a lot of traffic had passed on them. It was a worry, all these old rails. But I was the kind that it didn't do me down. I tackled the tanalith sleepers from the minute I was made Chief. We got shut of them. We had steady renewal with concrete sleepers.

When we started with the concrete sleepers, a mile or two is all that would be done. Then we had a programme of 24 miles, this meant you'd renew the whole system over 70 years. All the rest was second hand stuff or refettled track. Eventually we were able to make all our concrete sleepers in Inchicore at the Concrete Bank. Bob Spendlove was there. He was a great foreman. His father ran a private bus company in the 1920s. He used to tell the story how they would be out with their two or three buses and how they would cut in and pick up passengers at the stops before the official buses.

When we decided to ditch tanalith for good we increased the production of concrete. And then we moved production to Portlaoise and we produced very big numbers. It was a complete new factory built to our requirements with improved quality control. With concrete sleepers, we eventually improved the sleeper's size. It's a big sleeper now, but you need a sleeper that will not break.

We also had a plant which handled and welded rails. All this arose from the remanning and introduction of mechanised track maintenance, also in line with the better track, the long welded rails and so on. There were huge savings out of the remanning. The gangs had been huge in those times. We went to a six man gang, with two more if it were a longer inspector's division. We went to this straight away, if they got a bit of new track. We improved the ultrasonic testing system, but the mechanised machines broke our hearts. We could never be on top of them. They were breaking down continuously. The reason for breakdowns was that they weren't just machines, like a motor car, and they had this sophisticated measuring and sensing equipment. Then they eventually went to computerised equipment. You had modules, like, if something was wrong, the computer would tell you. You took out that module and you would replace it.

Denis Redmond epitomised what the chief inspectors were. They were totally dedicated. I always thought I got on very well with the permanent way men. A lot of the older engineers didn't connect with the men. They talked to the supervisors, they might talk to the ganger. But they didn't converse with them, they talked at them. However I would converse and engage with them.

Eddie Connor
Patrol Ganger, Westport, retired.

I started March 1960 in a permanent position. I was there years before that as a temporary man in 1957. I started with Inspector Jerry Lally. It was down at Ballyvarry on the Ballina Branch. The very first day I started on the job, I had an accident. A rail fell on my foot and nearly took the toe off. I got the workman's compensation that time; it was four pounds one and eight pence. That's what I got for four weeks.

You were lifting the rails using tongs. It grabbed the rail at the top and you were taking the rail in off the siding onto the sleepers. I wasn't so used to it. I left my foot in and the rail came down on it. A first cousin of mine, Pat Durkan, he was working on it too. I said to him: 'Pat, that caught my toe.' 'Twould', he says. I took off my boot and there was all blood and the toe was more or less hanging. Pat said to the inspector: 'He's in a bad state; he won't be able to carry on working.' He had a little pickup truck and he brought me to the doctor at Foxford.

At that time we were lifting the rails by hand. The rails would be lying along to be lifted on a rail truck. You got 30 men to the back of a 45 foot rail. Every man would have to do his job. If you made a mistake the rail could skew, every man had to pull his weight. Inspector Lally would say, 'I'll be standing over here and every man does his job'. He then said, 'We are ready to lift this rail.' There were a lot of men and one man in particular found it hard to move in. He just had one hand on the rail. The inspector said: 'Are we ready to go lads?' 'No', says Willie Ormsby. 'This fellow has only one hand on the rail.' Well the fellow challenged him: 'Why did you have to say that?' The inspector said: 'Any man that doesn't do his bit, he comes over here and stands at the fence.' It was a dangerous job if men didn't pull their weight. The men would be lined up. It was all 45 foot lengths and it could be 80 or 85 lb rail.

There were 30 men. They were figuring that the 45 foot would work out at one and a half foot per man. If you got a foot and a half of rail in your hand, it's not that heavy. You can fairly throw it up, a man that has any strength at all. When the men would line up, the first command was: 'Hands on.' 'Lift up', it came as far as the knees. 'Up for chest.' Then 'Fire' was the fourth command. Every command, the inspector drilled it into them,

On the miles (track lengths) you just had to keep the line packed. You'd just go along with two men. This was the miles, the maintenance. They'd have a long trowel, with a short length of blade and a handle coming back off of it. You'd feed the chips, about three quarters of an inch, in under the sleeper. That was the way the line was packed and pulled with bars. They had the 15½ lb soleplate and the crowbar. You got the claw of the bar on the plate. You got it in under the rail and it gave a grip. It would go away from you and sink down if you got it on the ground. There might be five or six men pulling the track. A man would sight it. When you'd be lining the track, wherever there was a kink, there would be the men out there plus someone to stand back and sight it, to see what way would they pull it. The best time to pull the track was when it was dry. You could sight it better.

On a renewal you'd spend most of the day and you would hardly have a bit to eat. You had to get in fast and get a cup of tea. You'd have a bit of bread in your pocket and you'd have to eat it out in the wet. It was a tough job. It was always said that the mortality on the building of the railway was higher than any job undertaken. This was at the beginning and men worked until they were 70 years of age. Some men were so interested in it, they still liked to stay on the job. Pat Staunton was 70 years of age. The inspector came out to him and said to him: 'Your services are no longer required.' And Pat said to him: 'What are you talking about?' The inspector said: 'You have to go home, your time is finished.' The next thing was, Pat fainted back agin the bank.

A lot of men who built the railway were taken on as permanent way men. My father was on the railway and my grandfather was on it. He walked the line from the other side of Foxford, down to Ballina and back. He walked twelve miles to work and twelve miles back. They had to be down in Ballina from six o'clock in the morning to six o'clock in the evening. He was 23 years with the company. That was from the time when the railways were built here. He had worked on the building of the railway and he died a youngish man. In those days they didn't have wheelbarrows to shift earth. They had hand barrows, with a man each side of it. There were so many men, there could be a hundred.

I retired on the 19th March 2000. I'm 74 years now. I missed the railway for a while. I enjoyed working on the railway. I did like it with the lads on the job, there was great fun at that time, even though the work was hard.

Bob Fahey
Patrol Ganger, Roscommon, retired.

I joined the railway in November 1960 . We started off excavating the
Ballymoe yard. There were eight of us. Two of us to a wagon. It was pure slav-
ery at that time, very hard work. It was throwing the muck up into coal trucks,
which were about eight feet high. I then worked in Knockcroghery. It was winter time and I cycled 16 miles to and from home. I was there for the biggest part
of a winter. It was tough after a day's work cycling home in the dark. We were
often drowned wet, and whatever misfortune was on me, whenever I was going
the wind was agin me, and when I was going home, the wind was agin me too.
But we were young and hardy then. I retired seven years ago.

The first pay I ever got was four pound one and eight pence. It was great
money. You got 20 cigarettes if you were smoking for the one and eight. And if
you went to the grocery shop with four pound, this room wouldn't hold all you
could buy. I found a man dead on the line once. He was trying to take cattle off
before the first train in the morning. I was walking along. I saw this thing in a
gabardine coat. I knew it was a man when I saw two wellingtons. I let out a few
shouts anyway. I went up then and there was no response. I said an act of contri-
tion. I went down across the fields to get help. There was another brother, who
came up. He looked at him and then stuck in the hand. He pulled out some sort
of plastic bag. He put it into his own pocket and went down the bank. We had
rung the guards earlier and they came straight away.

I knew all the farmers around. They'd be complaining about fences. If it was
Monday out, I'd say it would be fixed on Wednesday. We had no wire, no stakes,
we had nothing at that time. The fencing done then was only temporary, it was
no good for nothing. We had to cut sally trees sometimes for stakes. In the old
days you couldn't get a handle for a shovel. I went into a farmer's field and I cut
trees with a saw to make handles. The railway was a good job. There was one
thing about it, if it stayed raining or snowing for a week, you still got paid. If you
were working with a building contractor you only got paid for the fine hour. It
was a great company that way.

Paddy Hunt
Permanent Way Inspector, Castlebar, retired. Died January 2009.

I joined the railway the 5th of April 1955 in Ballinlough at the station there. Jimmy Cregan was the ganger, later he was chief inspector in Limerick Junction. It was fairly hard work at that time. It was all hand work. I got appointed quickly and was ganger of the relaying gang shortly after. I travelled all of the Athlone Division. Then I got the length in Ballinlough. I was then appointed A class inspector. Then I got Ballina. I retired in 1995. The job on the railway was regarded as a good job that time. There wasn't much else. Even though the wages weren't great it raised families. I missed the big relaying that came afterwards. We had kept the railway together on a shoestring before that. You wouldn't even get a new sleeper, not to mind anything else.

Every year we used to do some work up the Tuam line. We had somebody who used to make the tea on a fire. He used to take good care of me and give me the first mug of tea. We were digging out the quarry dust from the bays in the track and we came across this nest of pheasant eggs. They were on the point of hatching. We put them under a shovel and the heat of the sun hatched them. We brought the chicks home and a good number survived.

Mick Dempsey was the relaying ganger. He could exaggerate a bit too. There was a bit of a buckle. 'Jasus', he said, 'You wouldn't call that a buckle. That's not a buckle at all. You'd want to see the buckle that I had up at the Dublin end. I had to put a platelayer on my shoulder to take off the fishplates.'

There were big changes in my time, most for the better. We managed then without cars, computers, mobile phones. In the old days the inspector would travel on the footplate and he could throw out a note for the mobile ganger. It might be reminding them they had work on Sunday or something like that. If the inspection car was coming down, we'd make sure that everything was packed and ready. Everything would be tidy. It was best not to have any snap on the length. The inspection car kept people on their toes. Working on the railway was rough at the beginning, nothing easy about it. There was the odd row but most of the time there was good camaraderie.

Tony Marshall
'A' Class Inspector, Limerick Junction, retired.

I started on the railway in November 1967 in the Fenit branch. I'm from nearby here in Farranfore. There was scarcely any traffic, maybe just a timber train or a coal train, maybe three or four times a year. Plus beet in the fall of the year. Next thing, it closed altogether. This was in the 1980s. It's still there, it was never taken up. Fás worked on it afterwards but it's all overgrown with bushes now. We were there but I was shifted around; if there was relaying somewhere we'd work there. I have seen the Mallow-Tralee branch relaid three times. Later I got back into Tralee again and stayed there for a good number of years. I then went to the North Kerry branch (from Tralee to Ballingrane, into Limerick) taking it up in the 1980s. It was around 50 miles. They sent some of the rails out to the Sudan. An inspector came over from the Sudan Railways. He had good English. He was there for a week. He wanted to start at five o'clock in the morning. It didn't matter what kind of weather it was, he wouldn't work beyond two. That was his pattern. We sent 17 miles of rails over. They were loaded at Foynes. The soleplates and all went. A lot were 74 lb, as well as 85 lb. He liked the light rail, he had no fancy on it if it was too heavy.

I was patrolling for a few years, 54½ to 61 miles, near Tralee. We were shifted into the mobile gangs then. There was no man in Tralee, only walking it out to the van. I suppose I gave about seven or eight years above in the office at Rathmore. It was alright, that's where the relaying was going on. Lots of paperwork and plenty of overtime that time. All the older crowd that came in from the North Kerry line came to work here of a Sunday usually. There would be a vanload from Cork and another from Mallow. There would be a big team, near-ly 60 men. We'd do a quarter of a mile on a Sunday, all by hand. In later years I was putting turnouts together all over: Limerick Junction, Cork, and Cobh. We travelled home every night. I liked that work. There was a lot of travelling but we got over it. I had good men with me.

If you got injured, so long as it was small, there wouldn't be a word about it. It's a big difference now. I wasn't long on the railway when I broke my leg above in the station. A rail fell down on it. I was loading a wagon; my own fault, I'd say. I was back again after five or six weeks.

The old fellows long ago, they were very dedicated to their job. They took it very serious. There were two old men, two brothers on the North Kerry, and on the summer evenings, they could go out packing a joint. They lived in two rail-way cottages. And they could go out in the evening, the two of them, in their own time. The inspector that was here at the time, Jim Sullivan (he's since dead) drove to Lixnaw with a letter for one of them that he was retiring. He got, was it a week or month's notice, and he started crying. He didn't want to hear of going, he didn't want to take the letter and he knew what it was. I think a lot of them died quicker after retiring because they had no interest, it had been their life. You need some interest but they had nothing. There are fellows playing golf and everything now.

We had 'black weekends' in the cutbacks of the 1980s when you couldn't work at weekends. We had an inspector here one time, the late Paddy Byrne, and he'd be trying to 'whiten' the black weekends. A lot of the Farranfore crowd started in the railway in later years. We had an inspector here, he lived in Farranfore, and some smart lad said that he was better than a factory for Farranfore. He had a lot of the local fellows working for him.

At one stage earlier we had to break out the bolts by hammer. You could see bolts flying like bullets, with the head off of them. There was some kind of stuff in them that they'd go very easy. On a frosty morning, they'd go very well. There was something cast in them, they weren't the right iron at all. On a Sunday they'd put down a big fire and every fellow had his billy-can. They'd line up the billy-cans. They wouldn't drink the tea unless it was very strong.

The North Kerry branch was going well at one stage. There was a train a day, a mixed one. There was beet. Beet was more or less what kept it going. It was a good looking line. There were no tampers or anything. At a later stage they cut down the manpower altogether. There was maybe two men for seven miles. There would have been two men before that but it would be for four miles. It finished up with just one man. Dinny Foley. He had the possession, walking it. That was his job. They gave him a rail bicycle then. There would be bushes and everything so it was no good to him. It was a kind of a rail bike with an engine on it. There was an inspector in Rathmore that had a two-man rail bike. It was alright going down to Tralee but you had a good pull coming up.

I retired in January 2006. I was working up at Limerick Junction at that stage, an 'A' class inspector. I do a bit of fishing and farming. I'm happy out retired. I was hardly 60 when I retired. I reckon 65 is too late to retire.

Michael Baneham
Permanent Way Inspector, Heuston, retired.

I started in CIÉ in Pearse station, I was 16 and worked on the files. I learned a lot there. I then got fixed up with a job in Heuston station. That was in 1967. My introduction was on a Monday morning. I was asked to report to Gerry O' Mahony, permanent way inspector. There was a man there who was very small. He was the inspector's runner. He brought the letters and the timesheets over to the inspector's office. I thought I was small. But thanks be to Jasus there was someone smaller than me. I was about five foot six. I don't know what I am now but I wore out my heels on the railway.

I stepped into the office and was introduced to the inspector and shook hands. He had the biggest pair of hands. He had hands like two shovels. He was one big man. Incidentally he had the best pen work you ever could see. He had the runner and of course I was put up against the wall. Next he took out the measuring tape. I said: 'What's this?' He said: 'We have to measure you to see if you're ok to go on the railway.' I said, pointing to the runner, that, if he was on the railway, I must be alright, he was smaller than me. Anyway they did it as a bit of crack. That was my introduction to the inspector's office.

I worked with the gang who were out refettling on the Cork line. They were all Meath men. They had two Morris Minors, their own. There were no such things as vans then. All the shovels and all the jacks (which weighed a ton) were brought out by tractor and trailer. O' Mahony was a great planner. The shovels go here, the bars go here. In many jobs, you'd leave the tools in among bushes and of course the hopeful thing was that someone would remember where they were put.

Sometimes we'd pretend: let's say you hid away the tools last night. And you might be last man because the others were rushing down to get their cars. And you'd put the tools away and you'd find grass and put it all over them, as camouflage. Then you'd come the next day and Tommy Hetherington would say: 'Where's the tools Michael?' 'Jasus, I'm not sure.' You'd be only acting the mick and there would be murder going on, and someone would shout that the inspector's coming and then Tommy would shout: 'For Jasus sake, where's the tools?' And then of course, after a little bit you'd say: 'Here they are.' We had kettles; we had to build a fire. There was nothing like nowadays where you have the lovely little gas rings. You have all the facilities now; you didn't have them in those days. The man who boiled the tea was called the 'nipper.' The nipper's job was to look after the tea or if someone wanted something from the shops.

We were refettling on our patch. You'd be digging out the boxes and you'd have jacks each side. This would be in between trains. You'd be taking out sleepers and putting in sleepers. It would be French maritime pine and creosote sleepers. Creosote was bad to work with. Nowadays you'd have bags and bags of new stuff, as the money is there now. In the refettling gang then, we had to put in second-hand sleepers and we'd place them upside down. The smoother end would be now the top end, we'd put the plates on these, so we'd have to rebore most. It was hard work, it was go, go, go. You had a certain amount to do and the inspector would come out to see how things were going. We had the Robel power spanner then. That was very carefully watched. There was a certain person who used it and if anyone touched it he gave you a kick in the arse. And that was what they thought about machines in the old days. That was for opening the old bolts and tightening the new ones. We had a fellow in the gang, a man from Dunshaughlin called Michael Togher. Lord have mercy, most of these fellows are sadly gone now. We called Michael the 'Minister for Nuts and Bolts'. The reason was he got out a certain amount of fangbolts, only a few of these; they were a valuable commodity. You wouldn't see many of these lying around like you might in later years thrown here or there. This man had a job of refettling the old bolts with a wire brush and dipping in oil and if they were good enough they were reused.

I loved the railway. It was very hard. Very physical work. You never stopped work. You worked every day, even in heavy rain. You always had to leave the track in safe condition for trains to travel. Often you were out on jobs and you'd be, say, fixing bolts to a sleeper, you couldn't leave the job, you had to ensure it was safe. In those days after a while we got a square tent, a portable tent which would fold up, a few years later. Before that we had the old plastic covers off the old trains, these would go over some bushes. Many's the time on the railway I drank tea and the cup never emptied because it filled up with rain. I went into the office with the inspector then. I was still only temporary. Some men were kept temporary for ten years. It showed how good you were if they kept you on that long. Sometimes vacancies didn't appear. The minute a vacancy came up there'd be fierce competition.

It's a funny thing, a lot of railway men were great tea drinkers. The biggest tea drinker we had was a man called Dinny Redmond. He'd drink tea out of a straw. First thing he'd ask: 'Any auld bit of brew going there at all?' Anytime he'd come to see you, he'd smell the tea. He was the kind of fellow who'd sit down alongside you. He'd be the last man to leave the job. He'd know your name, he'd be talking to the new man: 'How are your family and how are you getting on?' A personal type of bloke, not nosy, but always concerned. That's why we had so much respect for him.

When I was offered the job as a timekeeper, naturally I read between the lines, there were people there, but I had read books, I wanted to get really into it. I started to fix machines and do things. I wanted to have my hand on everything. One would say I was a good acquisition, not building myself up or anything like that. I was only around twenty at the time, and they were looking at the future. I would have to say that engineers in those days, they knew about the present, but they looked to the future. They said there would be a better job, wait till you see how the railway will be a different thing. And they said there will be money put into the railway and we all went: 'Me arse.' There was no money in those days. It did come but who was to know. So I started as the time-keeper. The lads thought I was next to the inspector, but I wasn't. The gangers were higher than me. As I went feeling my way, I felt that I had that little bit to offer. The lads would come to me about different things. Some of them wouldn't be great with pens and they'd come in and say a letter came in and I'd help them out. I was working with timesheets and other things. Around 1971 Mr. Jennings came to me in the office and said to me: 'Would you like to take out a gang? Say six or seven men, start of with jobs like scrapping sleepers.' I said: 'Yes, that would be great.' I was married at that time and you'd always be looking for to be getting a few bob towards a house or whatever. Gerry O' Mahony actually fathered me, how's that? My father died when I was only 13 and he kind of took on a little role there. After work on the Sundays, we'd go in and have a pint there at Cleary's in Inchicore. Himself, myself, John Joe Mc Loughlin; he was a great relaying ganger. There was also the acting inspector, from Kilcock, a great railwayman and Andy Redmond. We'd have a couple of pints. Gerry would always take out a few corn beef sandwiches. His wife would make the nicest corn beef sandwiches you ever ate, with a bit of mustard on them. We'd all be looking at him to see if he'd take out the sandwiches. The inspectors those days had a big black coat. And he'd have the big soft hat. And out would come the sandwiches and we'd all have a sandwich each. We'd all have been looking forward to that point. We would first say we wouldn't talk about the job. And of course we were actually building railways. Sometimes we couldn't get the crane in the door of the pub. We had cigarette boxes and matchsticks saying this is the way it should be.

When the CWR started off I was involved in the stressing of the 'Golden Mile.' The Golden Mile was on a straight, from the 11 to the 12, between Sallins and Hazelhatch on the up road, 87 lb bullhead rail. That was really cared for and watched, to see what way it would react. There was a breather switch at each

Right. Labour intensive: permanent way men, armed with shovels, and train staff pose in front of a locomotive at Abbeyleix. (National Library of Ireland)

Right. The railway that never was: the 1837 plans of the Railway Commission included a drawing which showed a railway line to Berehaven, with the intention of allowing a connection with ships from America. Charles Vignoles carried out a preliminary study for this concept, which the Commisioners later rejected. The rationale had been that it would only take around 30 hours to London by this route, as opposed to three days by ship. (Iarnród Éireann)

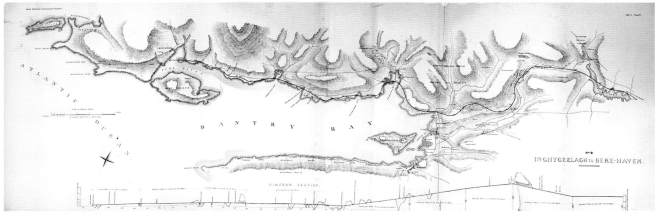

end. I always remember the stressing of that. There were the rail thermometers. They had the pullers on to stress it. I'll always remember. Roy Smith, the engineer, was out and Dinny was there as chief inspector and Gerry O' Mahony was the inspector. Roy was saying it's too hot, and then they wanted it to move a little under this catgut string which they used for measuring. And Dinny would come along and say: 'How are we fixed now, Mr. Smith?' 'Just another millimetre.' 'Here, I'll give you a millimetre.' He'd smack it with the hammer and the rail would run about six millimetres. I took charge of the CWR going in. It was all on a plan. This was the big push in relaying the Cork line and CWR was the new thing. It was all concrete sleepers. We started off at a place called Killian's Castle, at the 12 milepost and we continued relaying all the way up to the 17¼ milepost on the up road. Then we went from Sallins back to the 'Hatch on the down road. At that time it was 113 lb and then we went to 50 kg. We had all makes and shapes of rail but I reckon the 113 lb rail was the best.

In 1971, Mr. Jennings came and asked me would I go down to Navan and act as inspector. A man called John Maxwell was the inspector there. A very bright fellow, great with cameras and clocks, a real gentleman. I was a little bit reluctant, we had a baby just born, but Mr. Jennings said I could come back at weekends and work. So off I went to Navan. The inspector said he'd pick me up in the square. I was getting a provincial bus down. The bus was quick that morning. I got there and sat down on a bench in the square. This car came up and this man looks out, another man with a soft hat. A lovely smiley face. He passed me by. He went over to the busman and spoke to him. Then he heads over to me and he said: 'I'm looking for a chap called Michael Baneham, he was supposed to come on the bus. You didn't see anyone else did you?' I says: 'I am Michael Baneham.' 'Ah, for fecks sake, you're only a child,' he says, 'You're only out of your nappies.' I was very young at the time and very young looking. I had long hair. And he looked at me and said: 'Are you sure?' I said: 'I'm sure.' So into the car I got, and he told this story for years and years afterwards. So we went up to the office and he was telling me all the story about his division. And I looked out of the office at where the track was and asked where was the railway, those were only sidings. He looked at me as if I had ten heads but that was the railway. He said there was the signal cabin and all. So I went down and one might say it was a great experience. I met with different people and I was running the division for two and a half weeks.

I was brought up to acting relaying inspector. We were out there working and we went way ahead and I got a call from Portlaoise once, asking me to slow down, they couldn't produce the sleepers fast enough. I had thirteen men but sometimes the mobile gangs would come out and help, in the 70s. When the mobile gangs were formulated, I was then made the permanent mobile ganger in Heuston. Also around 1974 I became the acting inspector for Heuston when the job became vacant. I was out sick at the time. I got a letter to the house to ask me was I interested. Then six months later I took over as full time permanent way inspector in Heuston, where I remained and worked away and did every kind of job you could think of. I had an excellent staff. A huge amount of work was going on at that time. We practically worked every weekend to keep up with the work.

The permanent way is a big family. Nobody realises the responsibility. People think train-driving is a big responsibility. But the permanent way man is responsible for every train that travels that day. Not for one train, but for every train. And a gang goes out when there's a defect, whether it's in all weathers or all hours. They are there every time and they will never let you down. They have to go out and repair the track. If it's not repaired in a good state they are liable. They are answerable for all the trains. So it's a huge responsible job. So when you do work, you have to make that job right. I remember a manager over a different section saying once: 'The driver has big responsibility, the driver has to steer the train.' I said: 'Hold on, the driver doesn't have to steer the train, the permanent way fellows do. The track steers the train.'

Many times, when I was training for the marathon, I'd be dropped out at the 20 milepost. I'd use the railway as a training ground as well. I'd have my notebook and chalk with me. And I'd walk my length and train at the same time. It used to be terrific in the summer times. I used to put on the oils and got a lovely colour as well. People would say to me: 'Were you in Spain?' 'No,' I'd say, 'I got it on the job.' The rails would attract the sun. People used to think all the railwaymen were from Spain. In the summer, that was one of the best jobs you could have.

We were the ones who tested the high visibility vests when they were first introduced. We brought a gang of men down to Hazelhatch. And then the lads were told on the radio, off with the vests and they were all in their donkey jackets and you could hardly see them. It was a dusky evening and you couldn't see anyone. All of a sudden they put on the vests and the driver couldn't believe it. That's the first place they were tested.

During the big snow in 1981, the whole country came to a halt but we kept it going. I came out and the stationmaster, Ted Corcoran, came out. He had a pair of overalls. We kept things going as best we could. At the end, it was just four of us, Andy Redmond, me, Ted Corcoran and a shunter. We were cleaning the points and we got the last few trains in. Later we had breakfast with the Minister for Transport, I think it was Paddy Cooney at the time. A lovely man with a soft hat. I was introduced to him and I brought the lads that were involved. Then we had breakfast. We got great commendations. The bringing in of the trains was heroic, I've never seen anything like it in my life. We were the only station, Heuston, where all trains got in.

I was in Heuston until I came to the Training Centre in 1999 to manage the Infrastructure Training, which was being expanded at that time. John Cassidy was an excellent manager and the team were super. We covered the whole country. The railway gave me and my family a good healthy life. My wife and I have reared six lovely kids. And the money that I got, it was from the railway. I worked hard to get it, I can tell you. As much as I loved the job, I also loved the few bob. But it gave me a footing. And I can safely say this, the railway is the best job in the country.

Denis Grimshaw
Civil Engineer, NIR, retired.

After graduating from Queens University Belfast, I joined British Rail in Scotland in 1967. Looking back, I got a very rounded experience in railway and general civil engineering, which would be very difficult to get nowadays. The railways in Scotland have similar traffic densities and general layouts as we have in Ireland. After seven years there I came back to Belfast and was appointed Civil Engineer of Northern Ireland Railways. Short job titles were in fashion at the time, so I never officially had the title of Chief Civil Engineer as had all my predecessors and successors! When I started there were hundreds in the department, it was manual maintenance, with very little mechanisation. The entire track was jointed. There were eight permanent way inspectors, each with two gangers and about 15 men in a gang.

Just before I joined, the company had decided to buy two modern tamping machines with a view to mechanising maintenance. One of my first roles was to manage the reduction in the labour force to about a third of what had been. There was quite a buoyant economy at that time, relatively easy to get other jobs, a lot of the staff had been employed on short-term contracts, so we managed to do it without any compulsory redundancies. The only problem was that the number of people we ended up with, as had been pre-planned, turned out to be too small. It had been based on recommendations from people in British Rail, where the conditions were different: they had a lot of CWR and a lot of double track. Their manpower per mile only referred purely to track maintenance. It didn't include drainage, fencing, or off-track works. We struggled for a time with insufficient manpower afterwards and it was quite an effort to keep up standards. About two years after I joined, in 1978, I first put in an experimental half mile of CWR on the Belfast-Bangor line. I had experience of CWR in British Rail and had gone down to see the 'Golden Mile' on the Cork line before I did ours. We used 50 kg rail and they were welded in Portlaoise. We built our own CWR train and we used to loan it to CIÉ for several years afterwards. Our trial worked very well and we put in another three quarters of a mile on reverse curves on the Derry line. It was 113 lb rail at that time.

Then a major relaying programme started, about twenty miles per year around 1979. We decided to put in large-scale CWR on the downhill lines (where there was faster running) on the Wellington summit between the 59 ¾ milepost (north of Dundalk) and Poyntzpass at the 77 milepost. We put in 18 miles of CWR in just about a year. Our relaying was spread out among various lines. That continued throughout the 1980s. We had quite a number of major bridge renewals at the same time. We also had some involuntary bridge renewals! Some bridges got renewed more than once. It was a headache, the main problem was the general disruption to the railway service. It inconvenienced rail passengers and it really lost us freight traffic. There were some favourites for attacks. One well known one was Kilnasaggart Bridge, just a quarter mile north of the border. It had to be rebuilt a couple of times. I also did a lot of resignalling, replacing manual signal cabins with a modern centrally controlled track-circuit operated colour light system. Over my 20 years in NIR we moved from some 35 signal cabins to just four control centres.

We worked extremely closely with CIÉ and Iarnród Éireann. We bought a ballast cleaner between us. We paid for one third and were supposed to have been able to use it for four months each year, but mechanical problems often dictated otherwise! We did things to maximise possessions, on the cross border line, for example, one time we arranged to borrow the tampers and crews from CIÉ to augment our own, working in the same possession. In return for that two of our machines worked down south of Dundalk for a few months.

I moved in 1981 to Operating Executive and later to General Manager (Operations and Safety) – but with a return to civil engineering from 1991 to 1994 as the project manager for the Belfast Cross Harbour Rail Link and the reopening of Great Victoria street station and its new rail links. I left at the end of 1995 when there was an amalgamation of Ulsterbus and NIR to form Translink. The railway continued under new management.

I have worked in consultancy since. I spent two years in Greece working on upgrading the 500 km Athens to Thessaloniki railway, funded by European cohesion funds. This was transforming a single line railway into a double track electrified mainline, right through the mountains. This had involved some very long tunnels, blasting through solid rock. I worked in India for a few months, upgrading track work and resignalling in Mumbai. That's a phenomenal place – trains come in to the termini carrying 3000 passengers with three minutes headway all day long. I also did recent work on the Isle of Man railways.

Brian Garvey

Chief Engineer, Infrastructure, retired.

I started work in Irish Rail in March 1970 in the permanent way office in
Pearse station. I had an involvement then in the laying of the first CWR at the
12 milepost on the Cork line. I then moved to Rosslare. A new link span had
been installed there. It had been made for specific ships, the business was
expanding and my task was to adapt it for a wider range. After about six months
I went to the structures office; David Waters was the structural engineer. I
remember doing bridge design and an analysis of the Liffey Viaduct and the
Athlone bridge and a few other steel bridges. Then I went into the development
office where I worked on new freight terminals. I also stressed rails from the 12
to the 17 milepost for CWR, a big long straight. I remember, when it was completed, being asked to get on a loco to test it at 100 mph. There was a curve at
each end, it was on the limit for the curves, but everything worked. In 1979 I
went to Dublin Division as assistant divisional engineer, working with Joe Mc
Fadden, divisional engineer. There was one assistant divisional engineer post at
that time. I did three big bridge renewals, on the Cork line, in advance of laying
CWR.

I went to Athlone in 1980 as divisional engineer. The big issue there was the
very old track. The fangbolt was the predominant fastening. It was uniquely
Irish, brought in by the railway engineer, John Chaloner Smith around 1868. It
worked fairly well with creosote sleepers, but not with its successor – tanalith.
The tanalith in the sleeper corroded the bolts so there was no grip on the
threads. It was a big task dealing with these and lots of gangs were taken on, to
do re-fangbolting. The other big challenge was the bogs. There were 70 miles of
bog in Athlone division. Cross-level was a problem. There was a lot of move-

*Right. Clockwise from top
left: Installing a new
crossover at Killarney, in
February 2005. (Oliver
Doyle); welding gang at
work on the Cork-Cobh
line. (Joe St Leger); The
Donelli track gantry, supplied by Geismar; Ballast
train and tamper at
Portlaoise, 2009.
(Iarnród Éireann)*

ment. It was there that I picked up from the chief inspector an idea, that previous engineers had used, which was to use lime dust. We went with a scheme for putting in about two foot of lime dust under the sleepers and also drainage works. It is interesting that I learned 30 years later that a similar material, lime dust and sand, is used on the continental railways, under high speed lines, to give a solid and adequate formation. It was very successful; we got the vertical movements down from around 2 ½ to 3 inches in the worst areas, down to half an inch or less. This meant that when the CWR came, it could be installed over the boglands. Shortly after I went to Athlone, the first CWR came there, that was on the Portarlington to Athlone branch. It was the first in the west and then it spread very slowly. Another issue we tackled was the elimination of waybeam bridges. In general there were a lot of headaches with the maintenance in Athlone. I was really helped by the best permanent way man I ever met, John Cronin, RIP, the chief permanent way inspector, Certainly, without him, I couldn't have done it.

In 1993 I moved to Dublin as assistant chief civil engineer (new works), then Pat Jennings retired and I took over as Chief Engineer on the 1st January 1995. The big turning point for me in that post was the derailment at Knockcroghery. Two reports said we needed more investment. My task was to draw up a fifteen-year programme for the fixed infrastructure including permanent way, signalling, telecoms, level crossings, structures, overhead lines and buildings. The programme was drawn up, and eventually it was approved. Modern computer systems were also introduced at that time which were of enormous benefit. I got excellent support from Government, the CIÉ and Irish Rail Boards. We were given possession of the radial lines from Monday to a Friday, and then hand them back at the weekends. The production office, Portlaoise Depot and the three divisional offices performed in an exceptional way to exceed the work programme and carried it out safely and within budget. During the first five years programme, an unprecedented 100 miles of track relaying was achieved in one of the years. While I had direct responsibility for the track renewal programme, I did have the assistance of the New Works Department for the level crossing and other contracted works.

In my role as Chief Engineer, Infrastructure I had responsibility for the day to day maintenance of the entire fixed infrastructure. There were a large number of meetings to attend, both with the Board and with internal management. These were of great assistance in getting the position on infrastructure to the decision makers. However, I always insisted on getting around the system, more than once a year. Objectives I always had were, first of all, keep yourself safe when you went out on the line, to keep the staff safe and keep the passengers, who pay our wages, safe. I saw the first bit of CWR in the country on the Cork line as a young engineer. It was satisfying to see well over 90 percent of the country being CWR'd by the time I retired. The work is labour intensive and it was very rewarding to work with so many committed staff at all grades and who took such an interest in their work. I was 12 years Chief Engineer, that's long enough for anyone, time to move on, let somebody else in with new ideas.

Chapter 4
The Tradition Continues

The Irish railways modernised rapidly towards the end of the 20th century and the beginning of the 21st. Mechanisation, new techniques and significant investment gave a new impetus to the railway. Here, the men and women of the permanent way relate how the tradition continues.

Michael Browne
Superintendant, Portlaoise Rail and Sleeper Depot.

I started in Thurles in 1961, the 12th of October. That time, you were taken on for the beet season; you'd do up the sidings before the sugar campaign started. There were extra lads taken on every year. And then the relaying started. We used to clean out the boxes and we used to clean out under bridges with a hack and a shovel. That was the excavator we had that time. That was hard work but we were young men and we didn't care. We dug down two or three inches under the sleeper. We went down then to Limerick Junction. We'd work on throwing the muck into the wagons and then we took it out beyond the Junction and unloaded it.

Then concrete sleepers started to come in 1969, I think. The first job we did was excavation under a bridge with machinery, Number 7 at the 83 ½ milepost. That was the first time we ever saw machinery on the line, the first time we saw a digger and a bulldozer. The concrete was great for us at that time. We got lots of overtime from then on, that was the serious relaying of the Cork line. During those years we were constantly relaying. We worked every weekend. We used the Priestman crane to lay in sleepers and 50 kg rail.

The Donellis came in 1978. The first bit of relaying these did was down at Mountrath. They are a great invention. They work well. The first tamper I saw

Above right. Inspection car at Portarlington in 1942. Note, in the background, the old carriages, with roofs removed, laden with turf. There were many trains carrying turf to Dublin during the Emergency. (Father Browne Collection)

Right. Inspection car, Connolly Station, with Driver Seamus Kenny, 2009. These vehicles are used by engineers and inspectors to carry out regular inspections of the track.

was an old Matisa. I can't remember when that was. We had to jack up the track along in front of it. The first Plasser tamper we saw was an 04. It was amazing because it lifted on its own. Nowadays it's all machinery. I suppose in a way it's good. The road-railers are great, you know the lads that run on the rail. The only thing is we went off mad relaying. But I'll tell you that we should concentrate more on the formation and the drainage.

I became inspector in Arklow in 1978. Then, in January 1979, all of Ballygannon was washed away by the sea. I was used to the mainline all my life but Wicklow was second-class track. One time we got 85 lb Northern Ireland flat-bottomed rail and there was a hole in the flange of them, back about a foot and a half from the joint. They were the greatest bastards of rails. They'd break your heart, they kept breaking. Wicklow was a great old place, they were very decent people.

I went to Kildare in 1981. Then I went back to Limerick Junction in 1985 as inspector. You see, I had my house in Thurles the whole time. I had built a house there in 1973. I always wondered would I have been better off in Kildare, easier to educate your children, closer to Dublin. Otherwise I had to pay for lads going to Dublin. Maybe I put a lot of expense in going home. I still live in Thurles. I got the chief inspector's job in the Junction in 1990. It was difficult for a while. I had only done it now and again while Jim Cregan went on holidays. And suddenly you are thrown into it and you have nobody to help you.

I found it terrible for the first while and then you get used to it. I made friends. I met a lot of fellows, drivers that I used to know on the footplate going up and down. And then some of those drivers got foremen's jobs in Limerick and Cork. So I used to have no bother in getting locos or drivers. I got to know the signalmen in the CTC and got on well with them. If the boys below with an engineering train were caught by a train, the signalmen would always let them out, if you got e'er a minute at all. It kept the railway going, you built up a thing with others and you'd never be in trouble. We all kept it going.

I had an interesting time. On the railway, it's never a dull moment. There's always some little thing that comes up now and again. There's a lad, Eamonn Dwyer who does a show on Tipp FM every week. He drove me mad to go on and talk about the railway. He was tormenting me, so I went on and told them about life on the railway.

Working on the permanent way, it was a great old life. I found it great anyway. I reared my children. I got a living out of it. I built a house out of it. I'm happy enough now. You could say that it was all railway lads that were my friends.

Mike Devaney, Michael Flynn, Josie Ferguson
Mobile Gang, Foxford.

Michael: I started in 1966. At that time you were used to hard work. At home you were working hard lifting stones. They didn't believe in machinery then.

Josie: We used to cut the rail with a hacksaw. On an 85 lb it took three-quarters of an hour and you'd need to be moving. You'd have to keep it straight and keep pouring water over to keep it cool.

Michael: In the old days Fogarty was the stock taker. He would do all the stock. Afterwards they would go for a drink, the inspector and him. They went into Bridie Duffy's. And whatever was wrong with them didn't they bring the stock books into the pub. And next morning, when they went into the office, and they also looked in the car, there were no stock books. Some blackguard in the pub had thrown them into the fire and they wouldn't burn.

Mike: They'd be working below on the stocks and the inspector would be so exact. You'd get marks, and you'd be better to have too little stock than over and above.

Michael: He used to have a carbon copy then. If you were there and you were a ganger, he'd expect you to do three jobs. He'd hand you three different envelopes and there'd be a carbon copy in each of them. He'd tell you to go and do the work, like packing. He knew where everything was in his office, he had a chart up. There was no way you could hoodwink him.

Josie: If the inspector saw a farmer walking down the line there, looking at his cattle, he'd go down and shout the farmer off the line. They were big men, twice the size of him. They'd have to go back and walk around. They were afraid of him. He had authority and that was it.

Michael: If you weren't getting your due, he'd fight for you all the way. He had everything off and if he didn't know, he'd go off and read up on it. If you were dealing with him and you didn't have enough information, he'd stop and go away. Then he'd come back. He was a fierce man, but still we got on very well with him.

Mike: When I started in 1967 the pay was about eleven pounds fifteen shillings. There was no work around the place, only on the railway. It reared families, they were known as railway families. That time we were doing the Asahi down in the yard. All the Claremorris gang, the Ballina and Sligo lads were there. We used to work fierce hard. You couldn't be talking much. If you were laughing going out the gate at five o'clock, well, you hadn't a hard day's work done.

Michael: One man, one sleeper, pulling out. We were resleepering at that time and two men would hang them up. They would be putting in the new ones. they would lift the new ones in, the sleepers were shoed, one bolt on one side. You had to 'hand them, fang them and walk away from them.'

Mike: In the old days, our inspector, he'd be all the time rushing. He put the kettle up on a gas ring on the bogie and you'd be pushing rails maybe two miles up the line. While the kettle was boiling, you'd be pushing the bogie. And if it didn't boil quick enough, by the time you'd have pushed the rails, there was no tea. You'd get no tea until maybe one o'clock in the day. They were tough times.

Michael: You had to show up on time, you did nothing if you weren't in time. There were men who weren't taken back because of poor timekeeping.

Mike: Do you remember the times we brought the rails from Ballina, Mike? From Ballina all the way up to Manulla. We started early, at seven in the morning. And we were picking rails up all the time, you were never getting your load off. There was more going on all the time, we were pushing two bogies. It was fierce hard. It was a fine day but, I tell you, we didn't even have time for a pint when we came back. We were hardly able to walk home in the evening, we could hardly walk to the car.

Michael: There was great fishing in the River Moy at that time. The bridge gang were up there about 20 years ago. Some men from the area had put a net in the centre of the river. They gave the bridge gang fish and they were eating salmon every evening. You could go up to the bridge and you'd see thousands of them. It's not as good as it used to be. However, it's getting better. They have the nets gone and you'd see more of them. The drift netting is finished. They usedn't get up the river with the nets. Down at the quay they had two nets between the bridges. There were boxes filled with fish. It shows you the amount of fish that was in it.

Right. In motion: a Class 2600 railcar crosses Slatty Viaduct, in Cork harbour, on the line to Cobh. The reconstruction of this six-span bridge won the National Railway Heritage Award in 2006. (J. S. Mc Carthy Industrial Painting, Paul Tierney Photography)

Right. The morning sun shines on a new CAF Class 3000 Railcar at Londonderry station. The track on the Derry line has been upgraded in recent years. (Northern Ireland Railways)

Noel Armstrong
Safety Executive, Athlone.

My father was a ganger on the railway for 30 years. He and my mother had lived in a gate cottage just outside of Ballyhaunis, Hollywell gate crossing. where I was born and reared. He passed away in 1975, only 47 years of age. I started on the Mayo Line in that year as a platelayer and worked on my father's length. When I got married in 1976, I moved to Hazelhill crossing gate house. My children were born there, within a few feet from the railway! My wife is a gate keeper with Irish Rail.

In 1978 I did relief work in the Claremorris area in the miles gang and then I was appointed as patrol ganger. It had been changed to one-man patrols then. You patrolled twice a week. I got to be mobile ganger in Claremorris in the mid-80s. I was appointed to inspector in 1990 and was then appointed inspector at Claremorris. I was the inspector when the Knockcroghery derailment occurred. The reports on that incident generated the safety renewals programme.

I was appointed inspector on the renewals programme in the west. I supervised all the relaying there, this was the biggest amount of relaying that was done there since the railways were built. We relaid nearly 350 km in five years. I had four 'A' class inspectors reporting to me. It was a marvellous job of work that was done. It's all changed now. It's all CWR, there's no jointed track. The system of work has changed. It's all mechanical maintenance now, there are machines to do lifting for people, for hedge cutting etc. The manual side of things is gone at this stage. Most of the men are involved in protection duties now. The day of the shovel and the trowel is gone.

I remember the first time going out, Brian Garvey was the divisional engineer in Athlone and I was the inspector. We were putting track into gauge and reboring. I remember Brian coming down and he asked: 'How long do you think it will last Noel?' 'Well, it will last five years anyway' I said. In actual fact we had to get fifteen years out of that section before we got the relaying. There was never anything done with that track until we got the relaying in that location, in early 2001, I think. It just demonstrated the lack of investment that was there, we were working on scrap.

It's all mini-CTC on the Mayo line. The days of the signal cabins are gone. Years ago the signal cabins were a grand place to go into, it was like visiting houses, a lot of them. There was a big open fire and the signalmen treated them as if they were their homes, as well as their places of work. Generally in the west they were very friendly towards the permanent way. The ganger on his length would be in touch with them all the time. I suppose there would have been ten or twenty working in every station down the west. There would be clerical, platform, signalling staff and permanent way staff as well. Everyone knew each other. There could also be several generations of people working there as well.

We had a bad storm around 1988 when all the telegraph poles were knocked down. There was slushy snow, which built up on the wires. The weight of the snow keeled the whole lot over onto the ground. It pulled the poles out and the wires. I remember being out and the wind was blowing the wires onto the line. Eventually the line had to be closed, till the following day when we pulled them in altogether. The poles are redundant now. In the old days you could see where the railway line was from the road by the line of poles.

We had lots of bog formation down the west. We had various means of dealing with that. One of the first jobs I worked at it was around the 104 milepost. We had bog there. We put out a rake of quarry or limestone dust. We'd leave it out on the track for several months. Then we'd come along with the gang and we'd shovel the boxes between the sleepers. We'd come along later with the ballast and lift up the track for a full length and pack the stone underneath it. We had the long timbers then on some of the bog formation, to spread the load. The bog formations demanded extra maintenance. There was usually a 50 mph speed restriction on them. When a train travelled over this, it was like a wave going through.

There were times when you worked hard and long hours. I remember one period during the relaying when, for three months, I worked solid with few days off. I put in long hours which meant I was away from my family. I couldn't have done it without the support of a good woman. There were no complaints. I suppose she was born into the railway and was used to it. There were times you'd be gone for two or three days. By the time of that relaying programme, my children were big enough at that stage. I was there for the important years, when they were really small.

At Athenry. Clockwise from top left: Kevin O'Connor, Tom Grady, Tom Spellman, Stephen Gaughran.

Kevin O' Connor

I joined on the 6th of March 1990 as a platelayer in Athenry. The first morning I joined was down in the Tuam line, putting ballast under the tamper. After that I was involved in the relaying around Athlone for a couple of years, putting in new track and sleepers. I was involved down here relaying for three or four years. I suppose basically up along Woodlawn when we were walking it was all timber sleepers. We had a lot of work changing sleepers and broken fishplates and soleplates. With the relaying we got rid of all the timber sleepers and the old joints.

I worked my way up. I was patrolling for a few years, Attymon to Athenry for five years. I'm ganger here in Athenry now. I came in here when our inspector retired and I took over his post for six months, as acting inspector. There's eight of us in the gang. It's general maintenance, a bit of fencing; that kind of stuff. We had a lot of work recently renewing bridges. There were several bridges near here. We were out for about 14 nights, packing sleepers and getting ready. We get the tampers down now and we do a certain amount very year. Overall I enjoy the job. I'm a big hurling man. I'm involved with the juvenile team in the local hurling club. I went to the all-Ireland finals at Mosney in the community games. I manage the team. But the most enjoyable thing I am interested in is golf. I love it. I organise weekends away. It's a group of us at a local pub. There are about 40 members. We play all over Galway. My handicap is middle of the road. I'm working on it.

Tom Grady

I started 1972 on the Loughrea branch. That's all gone, that's disappeared. That was my first event; it's very hard to deal with, closing them up. It was running from Attymon to Loughrea, into the town, and there were people going in and out. But they made out there wasn't enough people travelling on it. There's a fine station house left. Then I left there and went down the Tuam line.

I was a platelayer there with a patrolman. We were two men; he was in charge of me. I was tightening bolts, packing and changing sleepers, making sure the place was there at the side for cycling down the track. This was a track to suit the permanent way men, to get from one end to another. You could bring a bicycle on there. That's all gone, it's all stone now. Ballast is every place. When I started it was all hard, there was nothing but shovels and picks and bars. There was no machinery then. We had a Robel power spanner then, but no contractors in, it was all manhandling, but I enjoyed it, we are still here.

I'm the patrol ganger from Oranmore to Galway. I saw no bad accident around here. In the last few years there were a few suicides around here, close to the city. It's not good, but you have to face that. Going back 20, 25 years there was none of that, around here. I'll be 37 years working on the railway this year.

Tom Spellman

I'm a patrol ganger. I started in July 1969. I'll have 40 years service in July 2009. When we started first it was hard going. There were hard gangers. There were hard inspectors. You had no say; you did what you were told. You'd see the chief inspector now and again. He'd be like God. The engineers weren't so bad. The arrival of the inspection car would be a big thing. You'd be standing there with the shovel straight. You stood there and gave them a wave and that's it. If they stopped you'd get a fright, you'd be afraid to talk to them.

I started out at Derrydonnell as a platelayer. I was in a gang for many years and then patrolling. My length is from Athenry towards Oranmore. I've been doing that length for 22 years. I know every inch of it. It was more interesting when you had jointed track. You were changing plates. You were looking for bad walls and bad bridges. There was more of a jizz that time in it. There would be loose fishplates, loose fang bolts. Now with the CWR and concrete sleepers it's all fixed, it's very straightforward. The fencing has improved now, it's all very good. Looking back from 40 years it was hard work. But I have good memories. People were happier that time, they didn't know any better. People were working six or seven days in the week. Wages were very bad. It was Sunday work at double time and it was very good. But it was hard work, working all day pulling out sleepers, using a hack. Pushing in rails with a big bar. Times are good now in the railway.

I remember one Sunday working down the Tuam line. It was snowing all day long and we were there with a cup of tea out on the side of the line, and the snow would get into your cup of tea. But you had to work on it, you'd be out all day, you had the line broken and you had to continue. In the old days there were no vans, people had to cycle 15 miles to work. You might have a bad breakfast and then take off and work till dinner time. You'd be hungry. They were tough times. The present day people haven't a clue how it was long ago. The relaying was a big event. I worked on that. Now it's all machinery.

One time down on the curve we had 140 sheep on the line. I spotted them and I couldn't get them off the line. I had about ten minutes. I ran up the line and I stopped the train. He saw me in the distance. I got my detonators and the red flag. I stopped the train just in time. They were on a curve and there could have been awful slaughter of the sheep. They were spread out for a hundred yards along the line. The driver got down from the engine and he helped me drive the sheep off. After we got the first out the rest followed. Sheep will do that.

I'm interested in sport. I like walking and I do a bit of swimming. I like cycling as well; I have a nice rally bike. I suppose being a patrol ganger keeps me fit.

Steven Gaughran

I'm a welder, based in Athenry. I work all over the country, mainly in the Athlone Division but in the rest of the country if I'm called. I joined the railway in 1986 as a platelayer and was plan patching below at Ballyglunin. That's on the Tuam section. It's closed at the minute but there are plans to reopen it, I worked as a platelayer for two or three years. I then spent a month in Inchicore on a welding course.

Down the years the defective crossings were a problem. You were trying to stem the tide, to patch and hold it all together. Now it has changed, they have changed to manganese crossings. With manganese the more traffic it gets the more it hardens, the more it's able to take. It's mostly manganese crossings with the relaying.

I travel on my own. Wherever I go the inspector would have men there to meet you, to help bring the stuff. A lot of the time you need possession. Some of the older crossings if you were building up the wing rail it could take you two to three hours. You can pass trains over it; you'd be stopped around ten minutes in advance to get clear. Most places where you'd be working at points and crossings, there wouldn't be that much speed anyway. It's not a lonely day. It's a great job, you get to meet everyone. There's not one in the Athlone Division that I haven't met. I don't think I've had an argument with anyone. When you get to know people you can have a bit of crack, which is all part and parcel of everything too.

I've been working about 22 years in the railway. It was hard years ago. The volume of bad stuff, the amount of time you'd have to spend on things. Now as I said it's not so much. I also have worked in Limerick Junction and Dublin Divisions. They are a helpful bunch of lads everywhere.

My interest is horseracing. We have horses. We have around four. Up to this we had one good one. He won a point to point in Roscommon, but he got hurt then. I get a kick out it that way more than backing horses. It's a great day out. I could look at a horse and see what's a good one. We breed them up from foals. We have three more that could have potential in the next year or so.

Brian Lucas
Divisional Engineer, Dublin.

I joined in 1980. After a few years I went over to Dublin Division, spent about six years there and ended up as assistant divisional engineer. Then I spent 12 years as production manager, this was interesting, right through the big relaying programme. Then I went to be divisional engineer in Athlone. I loved it there. The main tasks are to manage the maintenance in an economic way and get as much money for renewals as possible. I had good contacts from my previous job and I used to line up materials. Usually in October money would become available from unspent projects and, with the materials on hand, I was able to do the work in time. I got a huge amount of work done. I felt great satisfaction. At the end of my time in the division, there was virtually no jointed track left.

The most valuable time for me is in the inspection car with the permanent way inspector. The chief inspector may be there. Spending a day with the inspector is a day you learn a lot about the division. A day in the office – you don't learn very much. There's no doubt, the inspectors are all very wise. They've come up through the ranks; they know all the details about how to work and how to manage men – shrewd fellows. From my experience, the divisions contain excellent technical staff and inspectors, all part of enthusiastic and well-motivated teams. Here in the Dublin Division, the Wexford, Sligo and Waterford lines are in very good condition. Previously the Wexford line had been in bad condition. Other lines are coming up for attention. The job of a divisional engineer is busy, you put in long hours on the job, but it's satisfying.

I have a few stories. I once did a job at a crossing near Waterford. We had a man called the 'doctor', who was there to fix machines. It was long job, very exhausting. We were using a new heavy geotextile. We wanted to know how to cut this. The doctor said: 'Leave that to me.' He drew a samurai type sword, that he had in a sheath, and nobody spotted it. He held it up in the air, I remember the dawn sun was glinting off this sword; the sword was so sharp, he just touched the stuff and the sword went right through. He didn't have to use any force, it would have cut someone in half, it was so dangerous. It lifted everyone's spirits, there was a big cheer from the permanent way gang when he lifted up the sword. It was like some warrior film of old.

There was a district engineer in the old days. He was a man of private means. The story runs that he would arrive at the inspection car in his Bentley. A chauffer would carry a hamper into it. It would have a half bottle of wine, nice cut glass and linen napkins. When he was having his lunch, they would stop somewhere in a section on one of the quieter lines, and everyone else would have to get out of the inspection car. This meant that the assistant engineer, the driver, the guard and the permanent way inspector would all be outside sheltering from the rain at one side of the car, eating their sandwiches, while he had his lunch inside. He had a reputation for being a very demanding man. There was one famous time on the Ennis-Athenry line. He used to insist on taking the signal staff for the section. One day the signalman handed him the staff in a 'disrespectful manner'. So, he wrote a letter to the district manager complaining about this. Two months later, on the next inspection, when they rounded the curve at the station, the signalman was kneeling at the end of the platform, holding the staff out in front of him. The engineer just grabbed it off of him, and thought 'proper order'. Everyone else in the car was having difficulty maintaining a straight face.

Another time, a permanent way inspector was invited by the district engineer to lunch. 'O'Brien, I'm dining with the county engineer. I want you to come along next Tuesday.' 'Oh, thank you very much, Sir.' It was a big occasion for him, so O'Brien dressed up in his best suit. When they arrived along at the Grand Hotel, the district engineer pointed and said: 'I'll be dining with the county engineer inside that window. You stand outside, in case I need you.' O'Brien stood outside the window and, inevitably, it was raining. At one stage, during the lunch, the district engineer leaned over and threw open the sash window and said: 'O'Brien, come over here', asked him about something and then banged down the window.

Another story from the 40s or 50s: the then Chairman rang the Chief Civil Engineer (CCE), complaining about something. Of course, the CCE was an independent man of private means. The Chairman was commenting on something about the track and the CCE obviously didn't like this, he roared: 'Nonsense, Sonny!' and banged the phone down. Another time, he was sending an engineer across to England to do something and this fellow put in for £50 advance expenses. The CCE was completely puzzled at this and said: 'Has the fellow no funds?' Another time he was heard saying of someone: 'Surely he is not depending to live on the stipend he is receiving from the railway.' I think there were quite a few of these for whom the railway was more like a hobby than a necessary means for their livelihood.

Right. Rail-mounted steam cranes were used for bridge renewals.
A steam crane lifts bridge beams during the installation of Overbridge 5A on the Dublin-Cork line at Kylemore Road in 1954. (Iarnród Éireann)

Right. Renewal of Rogerstown Viaduct, near Donabate, on the Belfast line in 1986. Two steam cranes were used to lift bridge beams, in a tandem lift. Steam cranes are no longer in service on Iarnród Éireann.

Brendan Mc Cormack

Chief Permanent Way Inspector, Dublin.

I started in November 1974 in Kildare. I was in a gang of 18. The CTC programme was underway. It was temporary work but like everything else it progressed from there – I'm still here. It was tough work but I had worked on the
buildings, which was hard, and I was just 20 and in the whole of my health. I
stayed in that gang on whatever work, renewals and relaying. I was working on
that until early 1976. A platelayer's job came up on the length from Straffan to
Sallins. There was a railway cottage in Sallins vacant at the time and I got the job
and moved there. I walked the line and did whatever maintenance was required.
In 1978 the mobile gangs were introduced and I was offered a job in the Rail
Depot in Portlaoise, in the concrete sleeper factory.

I had always been used to working outdoors and it was a big change. I talked
to the foreman and asked if there was any chance of getting on the welding gang.
He gave me the job in late 1979. I was back out on the railway where I wanted
to be. It was mostly the Cork line, I was appointed then as renewals inspector. I
knew all the lads and the gangers that were doing the work. I was delighted at
the opportunity. I took to it. The work was hard but, at 26, you didn't mind
hardship. I also did relief if the inspectors went on holidays and helped them
with stock.

I was doing that up to 1990 when this consultancy assignment came up in
Mozambique through CIÉ Consult. So my family and I packed our bag and
went to Mozambique for two years. I was working at a depot about ten km from
Maputo. My job was managing the welding of rails and getting them out. They
had relaid the Limpopo line up to the Zimbabwe border and were rerailing it.
For various reasons the plant wasn't in production. My job was to get it working
and get the rails out.

When I came home at Christmas of 1992, Dinny Redmond, the chief inspector, was to retire in April. So I was interviewed then. In March I was told I had got the job. We had been in Mozambique for two years and the chief's job was a big job. Dinny Redmond was the biggest railwayman around. He still is, he is sometimes referred to as the 'real chief'! Nobody would disagree with that, including myself. So I came back and started in May 1992 as chief inspector in Dublin, and I'm still in the job.

I loved Mozambique. It was a great experience for my family. It was difficult and fairly hard to achieve things. For example, all our rail was in the port. To try and get it from the port to the depot was a nightmare. But you'd go in some day and succeed and you'd get a load of rails out of the port. We used to go up the line with our load of rails, Even though their civil war was over, there was a lot of banditry going on and we used have to go 50 or 60 km up into the open country. We used to pick up the army at the city limits. They used to call them the army by day and the bandits by night. The weather was in the 30s and all these fellows would be lying asleep on the platform when you'd pull up with the train. They'd climb on and you'd be ready to go and there would be AK47s left on the platform. Then you'd have to stop frequently, there would be women given lifts going to markets, they'd be on the rail train, all sitting on top of the rails. It used to take nearly half a day to get up to where you were going.

When I came back, it was tough starting. The big investment had started. You didn't get time to think. Every week and weekend there was something. We had three or four ballast trains every Sunday. We had a fellow who worked in the divisional engineer's office, Tommy Gerard, who was a terrific help. Tommy, Lord have mercy on him, would let you forget nothing. The divisional engineer was John Haughey, he was a great man to work with. The track was his God, he devoted all his time to that. Every Tuesday and Wednesday, religiously, we were out in the inspection car, going around the division. It was busy, between 1992 until 2003. I used to do around 35 Saturday nights in a year. The work in that sense has slackened off. It all got renewed. We got on top of the heavy end. Little by little the miles started to join up, and suddenly, almost without knowing it, they were relaid.

The softer areas, planning, standards etc, have come in. I begin to wonder how we could manage without the computer and mobile phone now. Those of my era will be retiring in years to come and we will have a new wave of younger inspectors. They mightn't have the same hardship of track but they will have their own issues. This will be new blood, they are good lads.

A permanent way inspector now – you could change his title to manager. He has a lot more issues than just the track: he has HR, planning, has to deal with contractors, farmers, even finance, he could be responsible for a million euro budget. I have enjoyed my time in the railway, and still do. I always challenge people who give out about it. There are always great people on the railway. Everything is geared for people to travel safely and it's great when you see a train going with thousands of people, travelling distances and getting in on time. You feel that you are part of that.

Pat Mc Carthy
Permanent Way Inspector, Rathmore.

I started in 1982 as a temporary platelayer in Mallow. I didn't come from a railway family, it was a first for my family. I'm from Millstreet. It's just over the border in Cork. We have good crack between the Cork and Kerry boys. You've a mixture down in this division, it straddles two important counties. I moved up from platelayer to mobile ganger in 1988. I was three years a mobile ganger in Mallow. Eventually I was appointed then as 'C' class inspector in 1991. It was all jointed track. If you got a broken fishplate you'd have to be onto it straight away. The sleepers then were coming up to 40 years old. There was a lot of work, problems with gauge and we had to resleeper. A lot of maintenance, trying to keep it together, really.

I suppose we were lucky then with the relaying. When it started off, it just went. We actually got 17 miles in the year 2000 to complete the Mallow-Killarney section. It was a lot of work at the time, nearly 40 or 50 men. We then got mini-CTC and we have axle-counters now. There were a few teething problems, but it's fine now. After the relaying, I'd put it this way to you: I can turn the key on the gate on a Friday evening and be fairly sure that, other than animals getting on the line, that there won't be faults on the track. Of course we have the railcars now, we used to have the big heavy engines. They are way easier on the track, there's no pounding, like the 201 engines.

We have a lot of crossings, I think I have 162. There's always maintenance on them. With the upgrades during the relaying, if we do a bit every year we'll keep them right. We used to have nearly 50 staff. There's only 20 there today. It'll probably reduce a bit more the way things are going. I know there's less work,

The job is changing a lot. Staff are different today. You have to be on the ball, with safety stuff. There's a lot more paperwork. I suppose it was later in life that we got the computer. The younger lads might be better on it, but it has helped. It takes a bit of getting used to but it's good for the basic things like e-mails.

Vernon Kiely, John O' Brien.
Patrol Gangers, Cork.

Vernon: I joined in 1986. I came in temporary. I started over in the Cork yard. What you see today is what we built. They rationalised the yard around 1988 then. We were the gang then for the tunnel. The tunnel was mostly done on a Saturday night, it was tough. After that I went into the gang on the Cobh road. I did the Cobh to Glounthaune patrol length. I went back into the gang and from 1997 to 2002 I was mobile ganger on a temporary basis. In 2002 I walked down to Glounthaune and now I patrol up here in Cork. It's a shorter distance to cover in one sense but there's so much criss-crossing of the track. You see a lot more people. I do about a third of the tunnel.

John: My grandfather was on the railway. My father was on it. I'm on it and my son was on it. I started in the Mallow gang in 1981. Then I got transferred to Charleville. I was put in learning to walk the road with the patrolman that time. Over a period, I walked every length from Kilmallock to Cobh. They left me go after 3½ years. I came in here to Cork in 1985 and I have been here to the present day. I'm in the up road gang. My brother retired two years ago and I got his job patrolling, from Rathpeacon, nearly into Rathduff. In the other four days I'm in the gang.

There was a funny incident, years and years ago on the down road. If the rail was a quarter of an inch out, you put shims on the inside or the outside of the rail. There was a big concert going on in Páirc Uí Chaoimh. I think it was Siamsa, it included John Denver playing. Our inspector was Bernie Callaghan. The concert was on at half two and we were all rushing to get to the concert. Bernie was putting on plates and he says to a man: 'Get me some shims', and the fellow thought it was Siamsa. Bernie said: 'It's feckin shims, not Siamsa!'

Vernon: The fixed lights in Cork tunnel only went in the late 80s. The majority of men who went in would only have had hand lamps. Everything you did in there was three or four times harder to do than outside.

John: As you know the bullhead rail is supported by chairs. There was this greenhorn many years ago, he had only been there a fortnight. The inspector said to him: 'I need a chair. Go and bring a chair on the bogie.' He didn't know what a chair was and the boys put him up to it, he brought up a canteen chair.

Vernon: I'm fourth generation railway. All the way back to my great grandfather. My grandfather ended his days in a signal cabin in Kilbarry, just outside the tunnel.

The crow was the railway man's friend. I remember in Cobh, sitting down in the signal cabin with the signalman, Frankie Coady, Lord have mercy on him. I'll always remember one day, Frankie was sitting there in his armchair. He was just after leaving the train out. Frankie was sitting down, looking out over Cork harbour. I'm sitting over in the seat, having a cup of tea. Next thing, all I could hear was a knock, knock. I looked around. Frankie took no notice. Then you heard the knock again. Frankie shouted out: 'Feck off.' I said: 'Who are you talking to?' All I could see was a crow on top of the handrail outside the door. He said: 'Keep an eye on him.' There he was tapping on the window of the cabin with his beak. Frankie would give out and he'd walk up to the crow and hand feed him. The best advice I got on the railway was from an old railwayman: 'There's always a train.' Don't go by any timetable, if you were out on a track, there was always a train coming.

John: In the old days there was a round sweet can. A man in the gang would bring in one of these and make the tea in it. There could be ten in the gang. He'd throw their tea, sugar, everything into the can. He'd get a big stick off the ditch and he'd stir it. It was pure poison.

Vernon: I'll give you a funny story. We were working up in Blarney one day. We used to have a fantastic relationship with the older drivers. We'd travel up on the footplate. You'd have a bit of crack with the drivers. I'll always remember, there was a driver, he was coming down with a light engine one day. Some drivers were great crack, when they'd see us on the line they'd hang out the window and give a roar at you. Well, this fellow came down that day he had the window open and he was roaring at us and all of a sudden the next minute the roaring died down a bit and all you could hear was the 'f' word. His false teeth were after falling out of the cab. So we ran over and put them into a hanky and he had to come back for his false teeth, and you should have heard the roaring from us.

John: A lot of people retired out of here and you could see on their faces that they miss it. Back around ten years ago or more, the permanent way was their life. When they retired, they didn't last a few years. Touch wood, now they are. When a man was leaving from Buttevant, he spent the morning crying, I couldn't believe it.

Vernon: No matter how hard you are, when you leave there's a lot of emotion attached, when you spend a long time devoting most of your life to a place. There would have been good friendships made.

Pat Higgins
Permanent Way Inspector, Athenry.

I knew nothing else but the railway all my life. My grandfather was a ganger down in Manulla with the MGWR. My father, God rest him, was a guard. He never passed the station without wrapping a few coins in a newspaper and throwing them out to me. I looked forward to the trains passing. My mother was a gate keeper there. Trains were our world. She raised six kids on it. I don't know how she managed it but she kept us safe. I have a brother, Michael; he has just retired from Claremorris two years ago. He worked down in the station there

I'm the only one left on the books, myself and my wife. She's working at a gate house down in Streamstown. I suppose if the gates go automatic in time to come, it'll be another part of history which will pass.

It was natural for me to join the railway. I worked at the station at Claremorris for a few summers. Then my introduction to permanent way was in 1986 when I spent a few years plan patching and I suppose I felt more at home with the permanent way. We were trying to keep the track alive. They were great men, sticking it together. It was heavy work, but we were young and fit and we enjoyed it. It was good. It was seasonal, from April to October. After that I went to England in 1991 for a few years and worked in construction. I supposed that the chance was gone but I came back and took my chance in the railway.

I started then again in 1996 with the permanent way. I had my first introduction to relaying and it was fascinating, compared with what we had been doing. There was the Donelli. The railway hadn't changed since I left, we were progressing ever so slightly and this was just a new thing down the west, anyway. We did a lot of that and then, of course, Knockcroghery happened. That was a serious incident. That changed things. The Railway Safety Programme came at the end of that. Ever since that date there was a big transformation of the railway in the west of Ireland. It was great to be part of it even though we were very busy.

Some of the railway was obsolete. I had slowly seen the railway die where I was born. I saw the rebirth. It was great personally for me to see money being pumped into the railways and you got a good level of morale out of it. The figures are there, there was serious amount of work done. It was unprecedented. The lads that were involved with it were fantastic. We were out in all weathers. We were relaying between Claremorris and Ballyhaunis and the gang were from all over, Roscommon, Leitrim, Offaly, Westmeath, Galway, Sligo and, of course, Mayo. We couldn't believe the rain every day, but you had to be out and do the work. Once the road was broke that was it. There were long possessions but you had to have it back in the evening. It was great. There were some great inspectors that time. You had Joe Stenson, Johnny Gately, Kevin Martin, and Noel Armstrong. Of course the chief, Seamie Quinn, was involved as well. We got it down to a fine art, then that's what it was, it was just like a factory. Everyone did his job and it went well.

That was great to see, and now we have it, it would be nice to maintain it. We have to remember, it's still a railway. It's definitely safer but you have to maintain it. Bad hours are part of the job. You could be called out at all hours or in bad weather. It's all part and parcel of the job. It's natural. The flooding is a big worry at the minute. With this global warning there's an awful lot of excess water, storms are more frequent. We have to keep an eye out. You have to always expect the unexpected on the railway.

I always had a great respect for the permanent way even before I started to work for them. They were at the coalface and its unseen work, they were never acknowledged. They are getting paid for the job but, I don't know why, they have never got the plaudits they deserved. Some of these have definitely stopped serious incidents. Beyond a shadow of a doubt, they were great men,

The older generation patrol men were fantastic, we all learned a lot from them. Men with over 40 years have gathered a huge wealth of knowledge. We learn something every day but we are losing a lot of experience. We have to keep it up to their standards They kept it together with very little resources. They had pride in their work, pride in their track length and pride in their job. They did a great job. That's the way it was and hopefully will continue to be.

Niall Lynch
Divisional Engineer, Limerick Junction and Athlone.

I qualified in 1984. I was abroad from 1987 until 1991. I was working in London, and ended up being contracts manager for a construction company working in the City Square Mile. In the early 1990s I got married and was hoping to get back. I had heard that there was a possibility that the railway might be expanding. Pat Jennings interviewed me; he brought me in one day on his own and said: 'Sit down there.' It was an old-fashioned interview. He was throwing six-markers at me: 'Sketch me something.' Pat was really sussing out, did you know what you were at. I came to work in production at the end of 1991.

Brian Garvey, the then chief, asked me to go down to 'the Independent Republic of Limerick Junction', in the mid 1990s, initially as a senior assistant engineer. And then as an assistant divisional engineer. The work in the division suited my style, there was a lot of bridge renewals, relaying as well as level crossing closure works etc. There was an awful lot of weekend work, practically every weekend. Gerry Fahey was the divisional engineer at that time. Gerry was good to work with. He'd trust you and let you go off and do the work. We perfected the art of renewing an arch bridge between the last train on a Saturday evening and the first train on a Sunday morning. We had a system of shutting the public road on a Thursday morning and having everything stripped, down to the arch. When we got possession of the track everything would swing into place smoothly. We had great help; we had Paddy Connolly's bridge gang, plus John Sheedy's bridge maintenance gang as well as the permanent way men. We would have it all done, the bridge in place within 12 hours, ready to hand up possession. We had an auditor from a safety study, by the consultants IRMS, around in the late 1990s. He was amazed at this. He said that in the UK they could take a shutdown for a similar scenario for three to four days. I said, we'd do it overnight. This man could not get his head around it.

I became divisional engineer, unfortunately, when Gerry Fahey passed away, from cancer. He was only in his mid-forties. He was a lovely man, a very decent fellow. We have great people working around. The bedrock of the railway are the good guys on the ground, particularly good supervisors. Our inspectors, if they had gone a different route in education, I'm convinced that they would be chief engineer material. I found in most cases in the divisions that there is very good camaraderie and friendship amongst people. There is great will there and great love for the railway. It's a privilege to look after people where they are interested. There are very conscientious people out there and they get lost in the ether. No one knows about them. Compared to a lot of other organisations, we have a very bedded structure of highly competent engineers, technicians and supervisors, all the way down to the likes of gangers and men. We work very well with other departments. We have very good contacts with the Operations and the Mechanical Engineers, and we have great support from the Signalling and Telecoms side of it.

Being a divisional engineer, it's a very busy job. You should ask my wife really, what it's like for her. It's a very demanding job, particularly dealing with two divisions. You haven't much relaxation. You always have things at the back of your mind. For example, if there is a relaying job going on at night, you are wondering what is the story, what's the temperature forecast for tomorrow. If its stormy weather, you are wondering will there be flooding. There are so many things associated with the job, between the track and the structures,

I have had the pleasure of dealing with some great characters. One was Paddy Byrne, permanent way inspector in Mallow, one of the funniest characters that ever worked on the railway. I remember one time around 2000, they amalgamated Cork with Mallow. Paddy went into Cork. The Cobh line was jointed at the time and I asked Paddy to keep a close eye on the place down there. The track runs down at the back of Fota. Paddy was at his wits end trying to keep the place going and the track re-timbered. One night there was a phone call made into Cork station, from Fota wildlife park. They said that some of the monkeys had escaped. They were out on the track and they were worried that they were going to be hit by a train. And that these were a rare breed of monkey, in from Africa, and had cost a fortune. The station rang up Paddy Byrne who lived up in North Cork. This was about 9 o'clock at night. Paddy rang the man whose number he was given and said to your man: 'What kind of monkey are they?' 'Have they got long tails?' he asked. 'They have,' he replied. 'Good', said Paddy, 'When they are out there would there be any chance they would change a few feckin sleepers for me? I'm looking for a good gang. Leave them there until the morning and I'll come down and pick them up.' Paddy knew that there were no trains until the next morning. He went down at 5 o'clock in the morning and he dealt with it, met the local warden and got the monkeys off the track.

Engineers at work on bridges.
Near right, from left: Bob Stevens, Denis Buckley, Neilus O' Donoghue at the renewal of Underbridge 186, Waterford-Limerick Junction line, in the mid 1970s.
Far right, from left: Tom Ruane and Eugene Fox at the new Ballynahattin bridge near Dundalk, which was constructed on the Belfast line in 2005. This 7,500 tonne structure was slid in sideways during a three-day track possession. (Iarnród Éireann)

Right. Members of the bridge gang, stalwart at renewing and maintaining bridges, at work renewing Underbridge 389 on the Mullingar to Sligo line, in September 2003. This is over the Royal Canal at Mullingar. (Iarnród Éireann)

Left. A Class 2800 rail-car, on embedded track, crosses the renewed bridge over the Royal Canal at Mullingar in September 2003. (Iarnród Éireann)

Right. I walk the line: keeping it safe, patrol gangers inspect all tracks on a regular basis. Single track, flat-bottomed rail, timber sleepers, over the Taylorstown Viaduct on the Waterford-Rosslare line.

Left. Road-rail machine at work on Northern Ireland Railways. (NIR)

Below, far left. Rail utility trailers on NIR, carrying ballast. (NIR)

Below, near left. Works train of the heritage Waterford & Suir Valley Railway. (Joe St Leger)

Below. From left: bull-head rail, chair and key; fishplate; modern 54 kg flat-bottom rail secured on a concrete sleeper with a Vossloh fastening.

Left. Clockwise from top: Coolkill Viaduct before renewal, around 1916 (IRRS); Bretland Tracklayer at the Mullingar Depot, 1920s (National Library of Ireland); Inspector Dan Donovan, Chief Inspector Jack Healy, 1972, taking a rest from lifting the track at Dungarvan (Dan Donovan); laying early concrete sleepers using a tractor, 1960s (Iarnród Éireann); taking up rails, Albert Quay Cork, 1960s (Vernon Kiely)

Right. May 1923, during the Civil War. Inspector O'Neill and gang on a damaged underbridge, Tralee branch. (Plumer Collection).

Below. Left: drawing of entrance to Cork Tunnel. Right: an early photograph of the Boyne Viaduct. The original wrought iron trusses span the river majestically. (Iarnród Éireann)

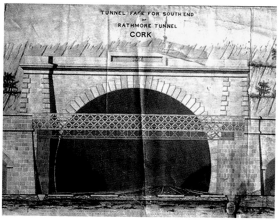

Huda Yousif
Engineer, Limerick Junction Division.

I joined Iarnród Éireann in May 2001. I started off working in the technical section in the then headquarters in North Wall, Dublin. I worked for Keith Chipperfield who was very helpful. Eileen Kelly was working in the technical section at that time and she took me under her wing and was of great help and assistance. As I live in Limerick, I used to commute from there to Dublin each day, 130 miles each way. My husband and children were very supportive and adapted to the situation. I left my house at 6.20 am and was back around 10 that evening. Because I liked my job, it was worth it. The work in the technical section included developing databases for stations and platforms in Dublin, Limerick Junction and Athlone divisions so it gave me an overview of the extent of the railway network and the geography of the country.

Brian Garvey, the then Chief Engineer, was very supportive and after about a year he rang me to tell me about the position here in Limerick Junction. It suited me very much, it's closer to home. Working in a division is good; it's enriched me with skills at various levels. What I like most about my job is travelling and driving around. One morning I could be inspecting a bridge in Knocklong, another I'd be inspecting a fence in Carrick-on-Suir. I get to meet a lot of farmers. I'd be dealing with issues like level crossings or lineside drainage. You come across the odd awkward one, most are nice. Even the awkward ones, they might be angry, but when you talk to them they are fine. When I go and meet farmers, they usually chat and ask me: 'How do you find our weather, is it cold for you?' People are nice and I'm delighted to have the chance to move around and meet them all. I know all the villages and towns over this region. I also deal with the local authorities, again good to meet people from different organisations. There

Right. The driving wheels of the Maedhbh, built in Inchicore Railway Works in 1939. Destined for the Dublin-Cork line, this series of engines were the largest steam locomotives built in Ireland. The permanent way carries the trains, as they evolve, safely to their destination. (Ulster Folk & Transport Museum)

Below. The Mk IV train-set, made by CAF in Bilbao, which operates at up to 160 kph on the Dublin-Cork route. (Iarnród Éireann)

are a lot of new bridges being built over the railway, so I also get to meet people from the Railway Safety Commission. I deal with my colleagues in procurement, production, and so on; so we're members of a big team, all working together. Niall Lynch, divisional engineer Limerick Junction, is a great boss and I'm glad to work with him and everyone on the team. I have worked on many bridge renewals. We just have had the ballast cleaner working here in the past week. Next Sunday we start relaying using the 60 kg rail. This will be its first use in Ireland. It's good experience, we attended a workshop recently on its introduction to the Iarnród Éireann system.

Railway engineering is unique; it's not a topic you cover when you do your degree. I did civil engineering in Khartoum and graduated in 1993. I then worked in the Ministry of Irrigation and Water Resources. The University in Galway was offering a fellowship under Irish Aid. When I started doing the Masters in Engineering Hydrology in Galway in 1996 there were people in the class from many nationalities; there was only one Irish person at the time.

I have three children, the eldest is a boy of fourteen. I took a career break after I did my Masters and stayed at home for three or four years. Then I joined Iarnród Éireann. It was a total change when I joined the railway, all the engineering was different. When I went to my work the first morning, I didn't have a clue what I'd encounter but I just went and did it. I'm delighted that I chose that career. When I joined there was much to learn. At the time I was trying to pick it up from other people's experiences. Nowadays, with the introduction of the track and structures standards, things are much easier. A new engineer joining will know from day one what we do on the railway and how we do it, which is great. It's good, we are all singing from the same book now. We needed these, with the challenges that we are facing now in the CCE Department.

Being a female engineer, firstly, it hasn't stood in the way of me carrying out my duties. The permanent way was a very male environment but because I get all assistance from my colleagues on the ground, from patrol gangers to the permanent way inspectors – everyone has been supportive and helping, so it's working out well. It's great, I didn't find any difficulties. They treat female engineers with respect. There are Michelle Lahart and Triona Heffernan, my colleagues, and the Chief Civil Engineer is female, so we're taking over!

I might've come across funny incidents. Me coming from a different culture greatly inspired the lads. So, when I first started, when I went to site a brave one (nominated by his friends) would come and approach me and start chatting away about the Irish weather. He would ask: 'Where did you come from; what do you normally eat?' I remember that lad who asked me: 'Do you drink Guinness?' He was puzzled when I told him I didn't. He asked me: 'What do you do at the weekend, so?' That was funny and now at this stage we all know each other and treat each other with respect – it's part of the Irish friendly culture. I have to say that my colleagues are brilliant in terms of respecting my culture and religious belief. I like it. After all, Iarnród Éireann is a very culturally-diverse employer with over 34 different nationalities represented amongst its staff.

Glossary

Ballast: Granular stone placed on the formation to provide support to the track system.

Bullhead rail: Rail section that has a head and foot of similar shape. This is now largely superseded in Iarnród Éireann.

Chair: A cast fabricated metal support for a bullhead rail.

Crossover: Two turnouts connected to allow trains to pass from one track to an adjacent track or to form a continuous passage between two parallel tracks.

CTC: Central traffic control. Trains are controlled from a signal control centre. As a result of widespread installation of CTC there are now few remaining local signalboxes on the Iarnród Éireann network.

Fangbolt: A track fastening that passes through timber sleepers. It has a spiked washer plate fitted under the bolt head to prevent rotation of the nut.

CWR: Continuous welded rail. Rails welded into a length, which, when installed in-track, is stressed so that there is no movement at the centre under the influence of thermal forces.

Fishplate: A plate used to connect together two rails at a rail joint.

Flat-bottom rail: A rail section in which the foot of the rail has a flat base.

Jointed track: Track that has standard rails joined together by fishplates and bolts.

Key: A fastening for bullhead rails.

Milepost: Marker placed at intervals of one mile along the track.

Patrolling: The visual inspection of track and associated infrastructure on a regular basis. Carried out by patrol gangers (colloquially known as 'milesmen' in the past).

Points: A unit of track consisting of fixed stock rails and moveable point rails used to direct vehicles from one track to another..

Possession: Special arrangements to control the movement of trains.

Sleeper: A transverse beam of concrete or timber used to maintain the track gauge. Sleepers carry the dynamic loading of rail traffic and transmit it to the ballast and formation below.

Tamping and lining: Packing ballast under the sleepers and slewing a track, nowadays done by mechanical means.

Track gauge: The distance between the running edges of the rails in a track. In Ireland the track gauge on Iarnród Éireann and Northern Ireland Railways is 1,600 mm.

Turnout: An assembly of one set of points, and other components that permits the track to diverge from, or merge with, another track.

Up and down: 'Up direction' means travel towards the zero milepost on a line. 'Down direction' is travel away from it.

Abbreviations:

D & KR: Dublin & Kingstown Railway

DSE: Dublin & South Eastern Railway

GNR (I): Great Northern Railway (Ireland)

GSR: Great Southern Railway

GS & WR: Great Southern & Western Railway

MGWR: Midland Great Western Railway

Note

A note on imperial and metric measurements. Mileposts are still in miles on the railway. Where people have mentioned imperial measurements in their stories, it is left as is. In other text, where appropriate, the measurement is generally given in metric units.

Bibliography

Arnold, R. M., *The Golden Years of the Great Northern Railway*, Blackstaff Press, Belfast, 1983.

Barry, J. W., *Textbook of Science: Railway Appliances*, Longmans, Green and Co, London 1878.

Boyd, J., *The Londonderry and Lough Swilly Railway*, Bradford Barton, Truro.

Creedon, C., *The Cork, Bandon and South Coast Railway*, Cork, 1986.

Cox, R., *Engineering Ireland*, The Collins Press, 2006.

Cox, R., *Civil Engineering at Trinity*, 2009.

Dow, A., *The Permanent Way of the LNER*, Permanent Way Institution Journal, Vol 126, July 2008.

Doyle, O., Hirsch, S., *Railways in Ireland 1834-1984*, Signal Press, Dublin, 1983.

Ferris, T., *Irish Railways, a New History*, Gill and MacMillan, Dublin, 2008.

Higgins, J. F., *Address to Chartered Institute of Transport*, October 1979.

Johnson, S., *Johnson's Atlas & Gazetteer of the Railways of Ireland*, Midland Publishing, Leicester, 1997.

Kennedy, M., *The LMS in Ireland*, Midland Publishing, Leicester, 2001.

Kerr, A. D., *Fundamentals of Railway Track Engineering*, Simmons-Boardman Books, Omaha, 2003.

Lee, C. E., *The Evolution of Permanent Way*, Permanent Way Institution Journal, Vol LV 1937.

Murray, K. A., *Ireland's First Railway*, IRRS, Dublin 1981.

Murray, K. A., McNeill, D. B., *The Great Southern & Western Railway*, Irish Railway Record Society, 1976.

Newham, A. T., *The Schull and Skibereen Tramway*, Oakwood Press, 1964.

O'Donnell, E. E., *Father Browne's Trains and Railways*, Currach Press, Dublin, 2004.

Patterson, E. M., *The Great Northern Railway of Ireland*, Oakwood Press, Oxford, 1986.

Rynne, C., *Industrial Ireland 1750-1930*, The Collins Press, Cork, 2006.

Share, B., *In Time of Civil War*, The Collins Press, Cork, 2006.

Shepherd, E., *The Midland Great Western Railway of Ireland,* Midland Publishing, Leicester, 1994.

Shepherd, E., Beesley, G., *Dublin and South Eastern Railway*, Midland Publishing, Leicester, 1998.

Sweeney, F., *That Old Sinner, the Letterkenny and Burtonport Railway,* Irish History Press, Dublin, 2006.

The Permanent Way Institution, The First Hundred Years, PWI, 1986.

Vice Regal Commission on Irish Railways, 1910.

Vignoles, K. H., *Charles Blacker Vignoles: Romantic Engineer*, Cambridge University Press, Cambridge, 1982.

Vignoles, O. J., *The Life of C. B. Vignoles*, Longmans Green, London, 1889.

Pictures and Illustrations

Pictures and illustrations are courtesy of the owners as accredited in the caption, and copyright of these. All other photographs, without accreditation in the captions, are copyright Michael Barry, 2009. Every effort has been made to establish copyright but, if the owner of a copyright wishes to bring an error to the notice of the publishers, then that copyright will be acknowledged in the next edition.

Index